# TABLE OF CONTENTS

## Section 1: Introduction

In 2005, the U.S. and 150 other states at the United Nations' 2005 World Summit Outcome agreed upon expanding early warning capabilities for possible genocide, war crimes, ethnic cleansing, and crimes against humanity. In addition, the governments and heads of states declared that each was responsible to use diplomacy, humanitarian and peaceful measures to assist to protect populations from the aforementioned four crimes. They also agreed that, if necessary, the 150 States would provide a collective action under U.N. Charter "should peaceful means be inadequate and national authorities are manifestly failing to protect their populations."[1]

On 21 March 2011, U.S. President Barak Obama announced the commencement of operations in Libya under the U.N. Security Council Resolution 1973 to protect civilians and their populated areas from threats of attack in Libya. This exercised and authorized military support to the signed Responsibility to Protect (R2P) for the U.S. Additionally, in August 2011, President Obama signed Presidential Study Directive 10 creating an Interagency Atrocities Prevention Board and an Interagency Review to directly deal with these issues. Obama related that prevention of genocide and mass atrocity was a core national security interest and the moral responsibility of the U.S.--military force, as an option, was not off the table.[2]

U.S. national security priorities have shifted since 9/11 with a focus on failed and fragile states. U.S. national security priorities sought to augment humanitarian and counterterrorism efforts through President Bush's National Security Strategy for those weaker and failing states.

---

[1]United Nations General Assembly, *Early Warning, Assessment and the Responsibility to Protect*, Sixty-fourth session, Agenda items 48 and 114, A/64/864 (New York: United Nations General Assembly, 2010), 1-8.b.

[2]Barak Obama, *Presidential Study Directive on Mass Atrocities,* August 2011, http://www.whitehouse.gov/the-press-office/2011/08/04/presidential-study-directive-mass-atrocities (accessed 27 February 2012).

Furthermore, the 2006 Quadrennial Defense Review encouraged partner capacity as a means to counter terrorism, insurgency, and threats by non-state actors.[3]

The core principles for the R2P are:

a. State sovereignty implies responsibility and the primary responsibility for the protection of its people lies with the state itself.

b. Where a population is suffering serious harm, as a result of internal war, insurgency, repression or state failure, and the state in question is unwilling or unable to halt or avert it, the principle of non-intervention yields to the international responsibility to protect."[4]

Two recent U.S. military deployments had these as their central missions: U.S. military forces and resources deployed for operations in Libya and central Africa. On 19 March 2011 U.S. military forces entered operations assisting international efforts authorized by the U.N. Security Council "to prevent a humanitarian catastrophe and address the threat posed to international peace and security by the crisis in Libya."[5] The intervention's purpose supported enforcing U.N. Security Resolution 1973, demanding the immediate ceasefire against civilians in Libya, calling them "crimes against humanity," and establishing a no-fly zone hindering Qadhafi's regime and supporters.[6] The resolution reiterated Libyan authority's responsibility to protect their population, "reaffirming that parties to armed conflicts bear the primary responsibility to take all feasible

---

[3]Lee Feinstein, "Darfur and Beyond: What Is Needed to Prevent Mass Atrocities," *Council Special Report* (New York: Council on Foreign Relations, 2007), 25.

[4]International Commission on Intervention and State Sovereignty, "The Responsibility to Protect," *Report* (Ottawa, ON, Canada: International Development Research Centre, 2001).

[5]Barack Obama, *Letter from the President to Speaker of House regarding the commencement of operations in Libya,* (Washington, DC: The White House, Office of the Press Secretary, 2011).

[6]United Nations, Security Council, SC 10200, *'No-Fly Zone' Over Libya, Authorizing All Necessary Measures to Protect Civilians,* 6498th Meeting (New York: United Nations, 2011).

steps to ensure the protection of civilians."[7] Lastly, the President emphasized Qadhafi's forfeiture and responsibility to protect his citizens, thus creating a humanitarian crisis requiring humanitarian protection and assistance. Delaying intervention would put more civilians at risk.[8]

Another recent case occurred on 14 October 2011. President Obama authorized a military deployment of personnel to Uganda providing assistance to regional forces in central Africa for the removal of Joseph Kony's Lord's Resistance Army (LRA). The LRA's actions for over two decades involved rape, murder, and kidnappings and presented regional security issues. The purpose of the mission served to "mitigate and eliminate the threat posed by the LRA to civilians and regional stability."[9] U.S. forces had permission to operate and deploy to Uganda, South Sudan, the Central African Republic, and the Democratic Republic of the Congo.[10]

U.S. interest in the four crimes (genocide, war crimes, ethnic cleansing, and crimes against humanity) associated with the R2P continue in importance; however, promoting conditions for peace and stability require early warning, assessments and vigilance.[11]

The United Nations General Assembly's Secretary-General reported upon the important considerations for the R2P in two critical areas: early warning and assessment. The Secretary-General called for more effective global and regional collaboration as a strategy for R2P. States and civil groups close to crisis have more details and access, nuanced information, and understanding of the historical and cultural pieces. Those close to crisis are directly affected by

---

[7]Ibid.

[8]Obama, *Letter from the President Regarding the Commencement of Operations in Libya.*

[9]Barack Obama, *Letter from the President to the Speaker of the House and the President Pro-Tempore of the Senate Regarding the Lord's Resistance Army* (Washington, DC: Office of the Press Secretary, 14 October 2011).

[10]Ibid.

[11]Paul B. Stares and Micah Zenko, Council Special Report No. 62, *Partnership in Preventive Action: The United States and International Institutions* (New York: Council on Foreign Relations, 2011) 6-7.

action and inaction. Consequently, they are key players in implementing actions.[12] "Context matters" and R2P must respect institution and cultural norms and differences from region to region continuing a dialogue on how to proceed, with government officials, civil society, independent experts.[13]

The report went on to explain that early warning by international organizations provided the information that enabled the regional and sub-regional actors to highlight and identify friction points that assist governments with obligations under R2P prior to the atrocities and violence. Early warnings assist with States' responsibility to remain accountable by providing the useful context and information that works within the developing system of international justice. Effective early warning provides insight into civil society. This assists with problem framing and awareness for internal and external actors and observers. Early warning assessments identify capacity gaps, create two-way communications, foster insights with stakeholders at the local and national level, and provide "uniquely valuable perspectives." However, their assessments should be checked.[14]

Distant observers sometimes have broader and "more balanced perspectives" into the "politics, profits, and national intersects" at the regional and sub-regional levels and at higher levels.[15] The interaction of "ideas, perspectives, and preferences" with stakeholders provided from early warning, assist with best policies and sustainable strategies leading to finding a

---

[12]General Assembly Security Council, A/65/877-S/2022/393, *The role of regional and subregional arrangements in implementing the responsibility to protect,* General Assembly, 65th Sess. (New York: United Nations, 2011) 2-3.

[13]Ibid., 3.

[14]Ibid., 3, 6-7.

[15]General Assembly Security Council, 7.

balance of best outcomes from the complex environment.[16] Regional and sub-regional actors'

critical role in information flow, when accurate and timely for analysis and decision-making,

assures the lessening of misinterpretations or distortions.[17]

The International Commission on Intervention and State Sovereignty indicated a lack of

resources devoted to early warning and analysis. Genocide and mass atrocity (GMA) prevention

means having accurate predictions; failure results in missed opportunities for early actions.

Misreading the problem often leads to application of the wrong tools and resources. Predicting

violent conflict has issues with the following: multiple variables; root cause of the conflict with

the complexities associated with their interaction; absence of predictive conflict models; and

accurate information for analysis and action.[18] Numerous third party actors, which include a

range of NGOs and international organizations, devote resources exclusively to the early warning

of conflict. Such organizations as International Crisis Group (ICG) report on conflict emergence

and aggressively alert governments. Amnesty International, Human Rights Watch, and Federation

international des ligues des droits de l'hommes (FIDH) monitor and report upon early warning

signs. [19] Effective early warning mechanisms provide accurate information and assist later in

prevention processes by giving "bottom-up learning processes" that assist states to succeed in

addressing the obligations of R2P, "instead of reacting once it has failed to protect."[20]

Third parties use different methodologies to observe and warn of instability, conflict,

war, and genocide and mass atrocity. Third parties' warning signs and indicators provide

---

[16]Ibid.

[17]General Assembly Security Council United Nations, 8.

[18]International Commission on Intervention and State Sovereignty, *The Responsibility to Protect. Right of Humanitarian Intervention* (Ottawa, ON: International Development Research Centre, 2001) 21.

[19]Ibid.

[20]Ibid., 5.

information, context, and understanding to possible mass atrocity and genocide events. The research question asks: How effective are third party methodologies to provide warnings and indicators to possible mass atrocity and genocide events?

Within the study, the third parties of interest are entities advocating for the prevention of mass atrocity and genocide. They include, but are not limited to, intergovernmental organizations (IGO), non-governmental organizations (NGO), humanitarian organizations, charities, aid agencies, academic institutions, or advocacy groups with an international mission for advocacy, awareness, and influence to the prevention of genocide and mass atrocity.

The findings of this research are aimed at an audience that includes the interagency policy community, senior leaders or decision makers in mass atrocity and genocide prevention, non-governmental policy advocates, governments, military planners, and those who implement mass atrocity and genocide prevention policy.

Third parties monitoring mass atrocity and genocide in high-risk conditions provide uniquely useful indicators and warnings of possible mass atrocity. These activities can be critical to U.S. efforts to meet its obligations under the Responsibility to Protect (R2P). Third parties, senior leaders, and military planners have difficulty in high-risk settings identifying indicators of mass atrocity and genocide and issue effective warnings. Warning signs and indicators must have reliable and regularly updated research methods of data collection. Logical and proven methods allow understanding, visualizing, and describing the situation in its proper frame and a narrative to policy advocates and senior policy-makers. Furthermore, proper context allows decision-makers to make informed decisions supporting obligations of R2P and increasing efforts preventing mass atrocity and genocide through plans tailored to meet instability.

The *Mass Atrocity Prevention and Response Options: a Policy Handbook* (MAPRO) serves as a reference for policy makers regarding how to deal with mass atrocity and genocide situations requiring monitoring, prevention, and response. MAPRO was developed to assist interagency members in the policy community to develop whole of government approaches with prevention and response for senior leaders dealing in GMA scenarios. Often the problem becomes one of policy maker inaction in the interagency information processing and decision making. Longer time for action creates greater risk for atrocity and human death. Inadequate planning and risk assessment preclude effective MAPRO measures. The goal of the handbook is to assist policy makers with process and MAPRO considerations to "digest information, develop a variety of options" and present relevant information to policy makers.[21] MAPRO is not a guide for military action but used to support decision-making actions, what DIME (Diplomacy, Information, Military, and Economic) actions to take, and how to synchronize actions in time, space, and purpose.[22]

MAPRO outlines guidelines that have universality. These guidelines have applicability when they use prevention instead of response, integrate the DIME tools, give situational context, use quick action for opportunities, address problems, are multilateral in nature, and plan transition and end state early. The spectrum of options ranges from inaction to military intervention.[23] MAPRO seeks to understand potential MAPRO situations to arrange appropriate responses, informed by "rational and deliberate assessments of circumstances, interests, risks, and prospects of success".[24]

The U.S. and international community have significant interest in halting GMA in the prevention of human suffering and human rights protection, which establishes U.S. legitimacy

---

[21]U.S. Army Peacekeeping and Stability Operations Institute, *Mass Atrocity Prevention and Response Options (MAPRO): A Policy Planning Handbook* (Carlisle, PA: Peacekeeping and Stability Operations Institute, 2012), 1-2.

[22]Ibid., 24.

[23]Ibid., 3, 5.

[24]Ibid., 7.

and credibility. Mass atrocity has global moral implications that continue long after the incidents complete and the U.S.'s interests may be in regional stability and preventing actors who commit atrocities, crimes, or terrorist acts.[25]

Information is a key asset for policy makers' ability to determine actual or potential GMA situations. According to the military's assessment of requirements for responding to GMA, indications and warnings are central and an overall weakness in the U.S. approach. The United States Government (USG) efforts rely upon credible information to respond, mitigate, or stop GMA. MAPRO supports multilateral effort, and their information, because it gives greater legitimacy to the U.S., segregates perpetrators and their supporters, uses the advantages that partners already have, and distributes MAPRO efforts. Multilateral early planning manages expectations, provides unity of purpose, and allows post and pre-conflict stabilization and reconstruction. While some countries reluctantly accept military efforts, they may be willing partners in early stabilization issues that build valuable partnership instead of military intervention.[26]

MAPRO's gaps deal with partnerships and information sources of GMA; mainly, on a method to consider and validate outside or open sourced information that furthers MAPRO strategies of universality in plans and policies. Also, MAPRO focuses on partners to provide useful information, but useful sources can and indeed do come from third parties who are not necessarily partners but have a stake in GMA prevention efforts. Facts bearing on the issues of potential GMA are mutually exclusive, so long as those facts are verifiable and credible. MAPRO does not address a method to determine which third parties provide useful information. The purpose of this research is to offer a method assisting planners and decision-makers to discern

---

[25]Ibid., 7-9.
[26]Ibid., 19.

what open sourced or third party information is credible and legitimate to consider in on-going MAPRO situations.

Military operational planners derive usefulness in a MAPRO lens because it promotes the U.S. interests in the conduct of activities and assessments abroad.[27] It also facilitates cooperation between policies and plans. Policy-makers want "flexibility, ambiguity, and the ability to keep options open" while planners "prefer as much specificity as possible regarding guidance, assumptions, resources, objectives, and constraints."[28] MAPRO helps to establish the discourse but the operational planner establishes context for the situations, deriving scenarios from sources close to the problem. Valid third party facts and information, warning signs and indicators provide the operational planner more options to consider. Those options might include employing means outside of military intervention. Third party information of warning signs and indicators assists the operational planner with developing a possible early course of action, which includes MAPRO strategies using time, space, and purpose. Additionally, verifiable situational reports and information become a useful resource for planners and staffs to corroborate their own intelligence and information or assist in understanding complex problems that require decision-making.

Military planners consider gathering and exchanging information with interagency planners for the development of plans. A network of working relationships and communications facilitates the whole of government cooperation required throughout the process. MAPRO's use in conjunction with the military planner's design methodology and military decision making process (MDMP) contribute to common understanding of the environment and the development

---

[27]Ibid., 34.

[28]Ibid., 22.

of relevant plans and actions to potential GMA situations, and corroborations of known facts and information gained from credible sources.

The research methodology used investigated the usefulness of third party GMA prevention advocates. It examined several third party methodologies for detecting GMA warning signs and indicators against criteria. The major questions asked are the following:

The question at the heart of this research is: how effective are third parties at providing useful indications and warnings (IWs) of impending mass atrocities or genocide (MA/G)? In order to answer this question, a clear understanding of what the scholarly literature identifies as the best indications and warnings of GMA is explored. Then an examination of methodologies used by cross sampling of third parties will be assessed for their abilities to identify, validate, and communicate effective warnings to interested audiences.

How effective are current methodologies used by third parties at providing indicators and warning of possible mass atrocity and genocide events?

1.  What are the accepted early warning signs and indicators of genocide and mass atrocity?

2.  Do third parties utilize acceptable methodologies for validating warning signs and indicators to mass atrocity and genocide?

Data gathered in the research came from third party websites to verify that the right warning signs and indicators were observed, that their methods for observing them were sound, and that those indicators provided insight (purpose) into predicting genocide or mass atrocity events. These criteria were compared for each of the third parties researched. The comparison identified if third parties had defined and understood early warning indicators. Also, were third parties in place or have the right sources to identify and analyze the indicators? Did third parties fact-check and validate their methods of observation? Additionally, third party methodologies were examined to see if they provided useful information for actionable options for decision-

10

makers and provide either prevention options or contextualized information or facts bearing on potential GMA situations. The third party organizations examined are the following: Harvard Humanitarian Initiative; Harvard Satellite Sentinel Project (SSI), Operational Satellite Application Programme (UNOSAT), Human Rights Watch (HRW), WITNESS, International Crisis Group (ICG); Amnesty International (AI); Federation international des ligue des doits de l'homme (FIDH), Forum of Early Warning and Early Response-Africa (FEWER), Genocide Watch, and the United Nations.

This research seeks to determine if third parties not only report clearly but also can analyze mass atrocity and genocide potential with a degree of accuracy as to be useful to the United States' interests in the R2P and atrocity prevention.

## Section 2: Indications and Warning of Genocide and Mass Atrocity

What are the early warning signs and indicators? What are the key factors within those indicators?

Martin Shaw, borrowing from Carl von Clausewitz's *On War*, explains that "as a type of social action, war can be defined simply as an act of force by an organized social power to compel an enemy to submit to its will."[29] While something of a consensus exists regarding the definition of war, the current literature shows considerable debate as to the definition of genocide and mass atrocity. For the purposes of this study, the MAPRO definitions are used:

> Genocide: Any of the following acts committed with intent to destroy, in whole or in part, a national, ethnical, racial or religious group, as such: Killing members of the group; Causing serious bodily or mental harm to members of the group; Deliberately inflicting on the group conditions of life calculated to bring about its physical destruction in whole

---

[29]Martin Shaw, *War & Genocide* (Cambridge, MA: Polity Press, 2003), 18.

or in part; Imposing measures intended to prevent births within the group; Forcibly transferring children of the group to another group.[30]

Mass Atrocity: Widespread and often systematic acts of violence against civilians or other noncombatants including killing; causing serious bodily or mental harm; or deliberately inflicting conditions of life that cause serious bodily or mental harm. [31]

The MAPRO explains that genocide and mass atrocity Early Warning and Indicators allow an observer to "suggest mass atrocities are imminent or occurring (or, in the case of prudent contingency planning, they must predict that such situations are plausible)."[32] MAPRO suggests they require identification, definition, understanding, and a mechanism for further analysis so that leaders "can make timely and effective decisions."[33] These early warning requirements enable research analysis of third party methods for observing signs of GMA.

MAPRO states that, "Although knowledge of warning signs is somewhat limited and each case has distinctive characteristics, analysts of genocides and mass atrocities have observed some trends."[34] Through the exploration of third party methodologies monitoring GMA, along with their field experience, and academic research on GMA, one is able to establish a set of consistent models and criteria that resonate with historical GMA situations and facts and offer trends that are useful as warning signs and indicators.

Using third parties for information is useful but their endorsement can also give diplomatic legitimacy to the U.S.; especially, in particular cases when the internal affairs of other states might seem like U.S. interference. Additionally, third parties offer operational benefits

---

[30]U.S. Army Peacekeeping and Stability Operations Institute, 10.

[31]U.S. Army Peacekeeping and Stability Operations Institute, 10.

[32]Ibid., 20.

[33]Ibid.

[34]Ibid., 12.

through access to areas of the world difficult for the U.S. to access or obtain independently.[35] Finally, third party involvement in the public good, through their services, and supporting conflict prevention claims to be "more cost-effective for the United States than unilateral action."[36] Third party involvement is considered an important aspect of the U.S.'s obligations under the R2P to act or intervene.

The essence of predicting genocide and mass atrocity recognizes the environmental triggers normally associated with GMA. Looking into future war or wartime conditions and signs gives clues to impending genocide. Understanding the current and predicted environment in which mass atrocity and genocide manifests, helps form the basis of observing signs.

Martin Shaw sees the problem of genocide and mass atrocity as an issue in future conflicts based upon past actions. Shaw argues, "genocide can be regarded as a particular form of modern warfare, and an extension of the more common form of *degenerate war*."[37] Degenerate war "involves the deliberate and systematic extension of war against an organized armed enemy to war against a largely unarmed civilian population. Degenerate war can be seen both in the armed conquests and aerial bombing of great powers and in guerrilla and counter-insurgency wars."[38]

When considering genocide as a form of war, the implications propose that information from institutions is valuable because third parties who organize within institutions provide actionable indicators and warning signs:

> War is thus a highly complex social institution. Taken as a whole, it is as far as can be imagined from spontaneous outbreaks of violence, even if it sometimes includes them.

---

[35]Stares and Zenko, 4.

[36]Ibid.

[37]Shaw, 5.

[38]Ibid.

War is premeditated violence, precisely the kind that is most illegitimate in non-war social relations. War is therefore highly institutionalized."[39]

Dealing with war and conflict, then, relies upon a context of not only the warring factions, but also the social dimensions and institutions surrounding the overall picture describing and understanding each particular situation and the potential to degenerate in a conflict into genocide and mass atrocity. If war is considered pre-meditated then those plans and signs of intent may be observed. Third parties offer insight into these situations of deterioration.

Conflict in the current operating environment may be recognized as an institutional problem. Viewing war in this respect--as an institutional problem; therefore, relies upon coordinating or close association and access with state social institutions that have the prospects of going to war. Those institutions have the capability and capacity for characterizing war or degenerating into mass atrocity. Early intervention or early warning consequently needs to address the social institutions with the capacity for war, and include other social non-state actor "institutions" that also have the capacity for war or violence.

Observers of mass atrocity and genocide believe warning signs are difficult to understand, and identify, because each genocide and mass atrocity crises has differed. Even so, they share common warning sign trends and characteristics. [40] The attempt to find general conditions and trends in warning signs to cases of genocide and mass atrocity contains variables that may not lead to mass atrocity, and according to the MAPRO, "at-risk situations tend to share similar underlying conditions" which include:

1. Past history of such [GMA] occurrences (particularly if accompanied by a culture of impunity).

---

[39]Ibid., 21.

[40]U.S. Army Peacekeeping and Stability Operations Institute, 12.

2. Persistence of articulated and non-articulated tensions or grievances (often including hate ideology).

3. Lack of institutional peaceful conflict-resolution structures.

4. Closed society (isolated by the government from the international community).

5. Poor/malevolent leadership. [41]

Just like other civil crimes, trends show that perpetrators required three things: motivation, means, and opportunity. Motivations, although varied, might be comprised of a desire for political/economic power, territory, or revenge. The strongest motivations occur when one of these motivations is aggravated by a perpetrator's loss of power. The means are the perpetrator's tools. Those tools might be the political will, plans, and the right amount of perpetrator support. Three general conditions create the opportunity for mass atrocity: crisis, mobilization, and violence. A crisis usually triggers the event, then perpetrators mass together, and finally violence occurs, "which may begin at a low level before escalating to mass atrocities."[42]

The point of trends analysis, therefore, is that unique cases of genocide and mass atrocity move through a "common series of stages" even while there are "exceptions to general trends."[43] Certain situations, such as civil war, show that atrocities progress without going through sequential stages. Gregory H. Stanton, from Genocide Watch offered, "genocide is a process that develops in eight stages that are predictable but not inexorable. At each stage, preventive measures can stop it. The process is not linear. Logically, later stages must be preceded by earlier

---

[41]U.S. Army Peacekeeping and Stability Operations Institute, 13.

[42]Alex J. Bellamy, *Mass Atrocities and Armed Conflict: Links, Distinctions, and Implications for the Responsibility to Prevent* (Muscatine, IA: The Stanley Foundation, February 2011), 12-13. "Mobilization" can also be viewed as a means to conduct mass atrocities, quoted in U.S. Army Peacekeeping and Stability Operations Institute, *Mass Atrocity Prevention and Response Options (MAPRO): A Policy Planning Handbook,* 13.

[43]U.S. Army Peacekeeping and Stability Operations Institute, 13.

stages. But all stages continue to operate throughout the process."[44] Stanton views the trends in

GMA situations to patterns or eight stages: Classification, Symbolization, Dehumanization,

Organization, Polarization, Preparation, and Extermination (See Appendix 1 for a detailed

discussion of the 8 Stages of Genocide). [45]

Lee Feinstein argues that genocidal trends are both historical facts and a current danger.

He contends that it is possible to identify *where* genocide will occur with some accuracy and in

general, terms that it will occur; however, it is impossible to know exactly *when* it will occur and

become an actual crisis. Feinstein argues, "there was a thirty-five-year backdrop to the 1994

slaughter of Tutsis by Hutus in and around Rwanda. This history alerted the world to the chronic

danger of genocide in the region. It also dulled it to the acuity of the crisis in the weeks leading

up to the killings in April 1994."[46] If genocide and mass atrocity are both historical facts

examinable for trends and part of the current reality, as Feinstein argues, then discovering

effective methodologies to examine their likelihood contributes relevance to the research.

Some trends unfairly frame early warning to policy decisions about military intervention,

which becomes a problem. This potential for failure calls for methodologies assisting in making

good decisions especially when a question of whether to use military force through forcible entry

is considered: "the failure to intervene militarily in Rwanda and the frustration over inaction to

the stop mass killing in Darfur has had the unhelpful effect of framing the issue of preventing

---

[44]Gregory H. Stanton, "The 8 Stages of Genocide," *Genocide Watch*, http://www.genocidewatch.org/aboutgenocide/8stagesofgenocide html, 1998 (accessed 27 June 2012).

[45]Ibid.

[46]Lee Feinstein, *Darfur and Beyond: What Is Needed to Prevent Mass Atrocities* (New York: Council on Foreign Relations, 2007), 4.

atrocities"[47] Trends, therefore need to address the different options outside of military intervention and contribute to the discussion of when military options are indeed a viable option.

Daniel Goldhagen addresses GMA trends by identifying them as eliminationism, defining them within political regimes and their societies. He believes that political leaders deal with political or social challenges with eliminationist techniques often violently opposing unwanted groups:

> They transform their countries into permanent or at least semi permanent eliminationist entities, dependent upon a level of violence, often institutionalized in extensive killing campaigns and camp worlds, far exceeding the conventional repressive measures used to control discontented populations.[48]

Goldhagen argues that the early warning signs of "modern tyrannies--which include nondemocratic regimes and formally democratic countries substantially restricting or violating political rights and civil liberties--have a substantial eliminationist potential."[49] Signs might be observed within this framework. Regional eliminationist politics seem less likely to occur today because of "countries' mutually beneficial integration with each other and their regions."[50] Goldhagen's predictions counter Feinstein, Stanton, and Shaw because they proposed that this sort of integration causes inherent conflict leading to genocide and mass atrocity. Goldhagen believed that globalization increased democratization of the world and increased learning in culture, shared outlooks, values, and norms.[51] Third party early warning signs offer feedback to both opposing arguments, so long as early warning methodologies remain accurate, and as long as

---

[47]Ibid., 4-5.

[48]Daniel Jonah Goldhagen, *Worse Than War: Genocide, Eliminationism, and the Ongoing Assault on Humanity* (New York: Public Affairs, 2009), 486.

[49]Ibid., 487

[50]Ibid., 488.

[51]Ibid.

the trends are observed with a possibility of understanding, then it is possible to analyze them as trending toward or away from GMA.

David Hamburg takes a retrospective historic overview of circumstances arriving at noticeable trends. He contends that it is possible to know about genocide and atrocity before it occurs and warning signs are present and useful. He substantiates his claims by stating that both Burma and Zimbabwe stood close to mass atrocity because they are "foreshadowed by severe governmental repression, flagrant and growing abuse of human rights, and hate speech--especially incitement by despotic leaders against vulnerable groups blamed for the country's troubles."[52] Hamburg, like others, contends that genocidal predictions pre-date the mass atrocity, citing Darfur as having indicators decades before the violence of genocide occurred.[53]

Hamburg predicts early warning by using relevant and reliable information. He says that approaches should have "empirical research to identify high-risk factors and apply a wide array of strategies, tools, and practices for preventing violent outbreaks of all kinds."[54] He adds a different view by combining historic trends with early warning and prevention techniques. In this manner he advocates for a way to indicate the issues, but also a solution that prevents and monitors them simultaneously.

The general course of indicators demonstrates and draws connections between genocide, war, and revolution, according to Hamburg. These events have the capability to dehumanize and destroy acceptable societal norms through social crisis. Several historical examples show warnings were present, observable, and foreshadowing:

---

[52]David A. Hamburg, *Preventing Genocide: Practical Steps Toward Early Detection and Effective Action* (Boulder, CO: Paradigm Publishers, 2008), 4.

[53]Ibid.

[54]Ibid., 5.

18

Consider the Armenian genocide, which preceded but peaked during World War I; the Soviet expulsion of nationalities that began during the ten-year Great Transformation, whose huge disruptions created a social havoc that increased with the German invasion in World War II; Cambodia's purge of city people, minorities, and other labeled hostile to the new society, which occurred during U.S. bombings and new enthusiasms about revolutionary victory; and Bosnia and Kosovo, where Muslims were exposed to ethnic cleansing and systematic killing against the backdrop of the disintegration of Yugoslavia and violent wars of separation.[55]

Hamburg believes the indicators of genocidal behaviors were known, just ignored in recent twentieth century documentation. He suggested that research indicates warning signs of genocide years before it occurs and that it manifests "under the stress of war, imperial conquest, religious fervor, social upheaval, economic freefall, state failure, or revolution."[56]

Hamburg reasoned that the discovery of warning signs to the actual genocidal events has a long duration, enough time to act, and enough credible evidence of a high potential for genocide. Signals or the early warning signs each have specific responses, options, and contingency plans to counter the impending danger. Each case Hamburg investigated proceeded with propaganda campaigns through political leaders. Mass media used available technologies and organizational structures to execute atrocity. Genocide fundamentally requires a broadcast media message of propaganda uplifting the state and argues for deportations and conflict with the adversary. Thus, genocide gradually assumes form when no entities exist to oppose the messages. The gap between actual genocide and indicators give the international community time to prevent. Opposition serves as a preventative measure.[57]

Hamburg recommends observing indicators from social or political elements following these trends: "historical grievances and enmities; recent or bitterly rankling social traumas;

---

[55]Ibid., 32.

[56]Ibid., 10.

[57]Ibid.

arrogant elites prospering in the midst of widespread poverty; poor governance; poor education (including strong prejudice); rapid political, social, or economic dislocation; colonial occupation; war; and revolution." [58]

Young Turks, Nazis, and Khmer Rouge gained a marked advantage during wartime conditions. They were able to "seize power, recruit followers, demand unquestioning support, inculcate fear and suspicion against groups they identified as dangers to the common welfare, censor reports of their own atrocities while they fabricated reports of their victims' crimes, and finally, to carry out mass deportations and slaughter."[59] Hamburg demonstrates that war provides the conditions for genocide, and any methodology that involves early warning ought to establish signs of conflict as a predetermining factor. Hamburg links the methods of early warning with prevention give several purposes that recognize indicators, monitor them, implement solutions, and track their effectiveness.

Shaw concurs, "most genocides take place during or around interstate and/or civil wars.[60]" The context of war (in selected genocidal episodes of the twentieth century) demonstrates a selection of genocides that were enshrouded by war (See Appendix B, Shaw, Genocide Episodes 20th Century). Shaw stated that there exists "three central connections to the state and war:

1. The genocidal episode was organized by a state, or a power centre within a state, that can be regarded as the primary perpetrator.

---

[58]Ibid., 34.

[59]Ibid.

[60]Shaw, 41.

20

2. The principal organ which carried out the genocide was the army in conjunction with other state organizations such as the police, as well as party organizations and paramilitary groups.

3. The genocide took place in the context of a war between the perpetrator state and organized, armed enemies (often, but not always, other states)."[61]

Shaw admitted that there were cases where genocide occurred outside the definition of war. However, in those cases, perpetrators were from states both militarized and having military ideologies, and recently had fought a war. Additionally, he acknowledged that perpetrating regimes were totalitarian in nature. The perpetrators were military or paramilitary types conducting genocidal activity. Shaw stated clearly that, "In no case does war simply cause genocide."[62] More factors and underlying root causes are assumed, and therefore early warning signs may entail unintuitive triggers. Moreover, Shaw argues that the connections between war and genocide "are not simply external or causal, but are *internal* to the character of genocide"[63] and that "genocide can best be understood as *a* form of war in which social groups are the enemies."[64] The extension of this argument means that early warning requires an ability to observe social groups and the internal character of genocide.

Ethnic cleansing has similar trends as GMA situations. Hamburg contended that ethnic cleansing as a term denotes forcible driving of a population from their land. Although similar in some respects to genocide, they have this in common: "intentionality to harm and remove a hated out-group. Whereas genocide is the intentional killing of an ethnic, religious, or national

---

[61]Ibid., 44.
[62]Ibid.
[63]Ibid.
[64]Ibid., 44-45.

21

population in whole or in part, ethnic cleaning is the attempt to remove a people and every trace of their existence from a given territory"[65].

Hamburg believed that ethnic cleansing and genocide share the goal to "dispose of the 'alien' and claim their lands and goods" and ethnic cleansing eventually turns into genocide getting rid of unwanted and resistant people.[66] Ethnic cleansing or the deportation of the unwanted "other" precedes genocide, often by years in advance relaying an important indicator for genocide. The signs of ethnic cleansing have roots in human rights and dignity, and tolerance of racial groups. [67]

Common elements signaling ethnic cleansing included: "nationalistic violence, war, totality of displacement, destruction of monuments and memory, theft of property, and gender discrimination."[68] Ethnic cleansing relies upon an armed perpetrator against an unarmed victim.[69] These elements have particular utility in identifying early warning.

Ethnic cleansing occurs during a war or interwar, between war and peace. War provides the cover-up and an excuse for dealing with the oppressed minority. States often blame and target victims as supporting a state's enemy. For example, Young Turks (nationalistic political party in Turkey) during World War I, accused the Armenians of supporting their Russian enemy. This was enough justification to export Armenians from their homeland. The Nazis accused the Jews of supporting bolshevism and capitalism. After World War II, Czechs and Poles believed that stability rested in the expulsion of the minority of Germans. Stalin and Lavrenty Beria expelled

---

[65]Hamburg, 26.

[66]Ibid.

[67]Ibid.

[68]Ibid., 27.

[69]Ibid.

Chechens-Ingus and the Crimean Tartars arguing they backed the Nazis; hiding the fact that they were on oil rich land wanted by the government. Moreover, Serbs within the Bosnian war, wanted security and protection of their lines of communication and supplies, and adopted ethnic cleansing as their means to that end.[70] These signs give indication of impending ethnic cleansing and become part of building a narrative about violence and ethnic cleansing.

This section provided main ideas of useful GMA early warning and indicators that will guide an operational planner and policy-maker for early action and identification. Warning signs require identification, definition, understanding, and assist in prediction and analysis in GMA situations. GMA trends are similar to those of imminent war, wartime conditions, revolution, conflict over scarce resources, political upheaval or transitions, war of an armed aggressor against civilians, past history of GMA, closed societies, hate ideology and grievances, poor state leadership, and human rights abuses. GMA is a historical reality for which trends exist in today's operational environment, are observable with relevant and reliable information, and offer time between the indicators and actual GMA occurrences for preventive options using whole of government approaches.

## Section 3. Third Party Methodology

Uncovering indicators and warning signs of mass atrocity and genocide by looking at third party methodologies provides an array of examples, trends, and information that can assist in predicting the outbreak. There are several approaches to mass atrocity and genocide early warning. They range from prevention, alerting to possible conflict, or seeking peaceful resolutions to impending conflict signs. Averting conflict in the first place heads off mass atrocity and genocide indirectly. Third parties advocating against genocide and atrocity use suasion and

---

[70]Ibid.

compellence in early warning to not only prevent but also influence the conduct of war and conflict when and if they occur. If conflict should occur, then suasion and compellence through information from early warning methodologies and techniques assist to deter genocide and mass atrocity from characterizing conflict.

This section examines third party methodologies for identifying indicators to mass atrocity and genocide. Data was gathered to verify which signs were being observed, the methods for observing them, and that those indicators provided insight (purpose) into predicting genocide or mass atrocity events. A summary of third parties researched follows to give the reader an understanding of the missions, agendas, and methods used by third parties. Refer to Appendix C, Research of Third Party Methodologies; and Appendix E, Analysis of Third Party Early Warning Signs and Purpose, for data and detailed discussion of research pertaining to third party methodologies, early warning signs observed, and their purposes. Only a summary of the purposes and methodologies is presented here.

The proper starting point is the United Nations (UN), Special Adviser on the Prevention of Genocide because the definitions of genocide and mass atrocity, their human rights programs, and the Responsibility to Protect generate from the UN. The UN takes the lead on methodologies and analysis frameworks; however, they are obviously not the only implementing international organization for early warning and indicators of conflict, instability, genocide, and mass atrocity.

## United Nations

The United Nations, Special Adviser on the Prevention of Genocide uses a clear methodology that forms within the responsibilities of the office. The UN Special Adviser on the Prevention of Genocide (OSAPG) methodology is the standard for early warning of genocide and mass atrocity. The responsibilities of the Special Adviser on the Prevention of Genocide's are to collect and enhance upon existing UN information systems and act as a mechanism of early warning to the Security Council to prevent or halt genocide when related to genocide or their related crimes.[71]

The Office's Analysis Framework developed to determine the genocide risk in given situations and encourages others to adopt this framework and analysis. The UN list identifies the consensus of indicators and early warning from the literature review, and demonstrates the most important information that policy-makers and planners need in a timely fashion. The eight factors, which cumulatively increase the risk of genocide over time and the triggering factors follow:

1. Tense inter-group relations, including a record of discrimination and/or other human rights violations committed against a group;

2. Weak institutional capacity to prevent genocide, such as the lack of an independent judiciary, ineffective national human rights institutions, the absence of international actors capable of protecting vulnerable groups, a lack of impartial security forces and media;

3. The presence of illegal arms and armed elements;

4. Underlying political, economic, military or other motivation to target a group;

5. Circumstances that facilitate perpetration of genocide, such as a sudden or gradual strengthening of the military or security apparatus;

6. Acts that could be elements of genocide, such as such as killings, abduction and disappearances, torture, rape and sexual violence, 'ethnic cleansing' or pogroms or

---

[71]Office of the Special Adviser on the Prevention of Genocide, "Overview of OSAPG," http://www.un.org/en/preventgenocide/adviser/pdf/osapg_overview.pdf (accessed 16 August 2012).

the deliberate deprivation of food; evidence of the 'intent to destroy in whole or in part;

7. Triggering factors, such as elections.[72]

## Sentinel Satellite Project

The Sentinel Satellite Project (SSP) focuses in Sudan and their methodology uses "commercial satellite imagery, academic analysis, and advocacy to promote human rights in Sudan and South Sudan and serve as an early warning system for impending crisis."[73] The Satellite Sentinel Project synthesizes evidence from satellite imagery, data pattern analysis, and ground sourcing to produce reports. Specifically the SSP monitors six areas of crisis and documenting:

1. Bombardment and Attacks

2. Early Warning of Attacks on Civilians

3. Evidence of Apparent Mass Graves

4. Evidence of Forced Displacement

5. Tracking Compliance in the Sudans

6. Village Razings

Their purpose is to alert the public, press, policymakers, major news organizations, and social media; especially, Twitter and Facebook. They observe alleged atrocity as it develops and unfolds and "document, deter, and seek accountability for war criminals and mass atrocities."[74]

---

[72]Office of the Special Adviser on the Prevention of Genocide.

[73]Satellite Sentinel Project, "Our Story," http://satsentinel.org/our-story/partner-organizations#enough (accessed 3 August 2012).

[74]Satellite Sentinel Project, "Documenting the Crisis," http://satsentinel.org/documenting-the-crisis, (accessed 3 August 2012).

## Operational Satellite Application Programme (UNOSAT)

United Nations Institute for Training and Research (UNITAR) Operational Satellite Application Programme (UNOSAT) has used the technology in case studies in Libya, South Sudan, Krgyzstan, and Sri Lanka. Their methodology uses preliminary research prior to conflict mapping and tracking. Then it obtains baseline information pertaining to geographic security issues, and then identifies areas of interest to acquire satellite imagery data, followed by analysis.[75]

UNOSAT believes that geographic analysis positively affects "processes, initiatives and organizations with a mission to protect human rights and uphold international humanitarian law, thus improving overall human security internationally."[76] The contribution of the system has human security application in these five areas: advocacy, mitigation and prevention, enhancing field investigations, remote fact finding, and peace and reconciliation.[77]

## WITNESS

WITNESS is an international nonprofit organization with 20 years of experience in using the power of video and storytelling, working with 300 human rights groups, and 80 countries. WITNESS's methodology uses videos and storytelling to expose the world to human rights abuses.[78] WITNESS uses bystander captured evidence to human rights activists around the world, and now uses a comprehensive training approach focusing on video advocacy. Their program

---

[75]United Nations Institute for Training and Research, *UNOSAT Brief: Satellite Applications for Human Security* (Washington, DC: UNITAR, 2011), 9.

[76]Ibid., 5.

[77]Ibid.

[78]WITNESS, "About Us: Our Mission," http://www.witness.org/about-us (accessed 12 August 2012).

called, "Cameras everywhere" gives bystanders throughout the world the means for reporting human rights abuses. Moreover, WITNESS puts their unique video advocacy resources online, so they are adoptable and accessible to citizens around the world.[79] Their purposes are the following: activism as a tool for change, empowering and exposing injustice, empower activists to protect and defend human rights.[80] Also, WITNESS documents human rights violations, and ensures transparency, good governance, and accountability are upheld within society.[81]

## Amnesty International

Amnesty International monitors human rights in more than 150 countries. They have research teams based in London who conduct investigative missions throughout the world and publish an Annual Report summarizing Amnesty's work. Amnesty International uses three tactics in their methodology: research; action; and advocacy. Their use of independent reports uses rigorous research. They claim that they are undisturbed by corporate and government influence which adds to their credibility. In action, Amnesty uses campaigns and long-term casework to influence human rights concerns using stories of at-risk individuals and reports this to the international media. Amnesty uses a program called Science for Human Rights. This program uses technological advances in science to advocate human rights campaigns. They use geospatial technology, such as satellite imagery, to monitor human rights violations and conflict prevention.

---

[79]Ibid.

[80]WITNESS, *Cameras Everywhere: Current challenges and opportunities at the intersection of human rights, video and technology. Human Rights Video and Technology* (Brooklyn: WITNESS, 2011), 8.

[81]Ibid., 10.

These allow access to inaccessible conflict zones, show visual evidence, and present information in new ways.[82]

Their purposes are the following:

1.  To unite people to fight for human rights using three tactics: research; action; and advocacy.

2.  Publish independent reports based upon rigorous research, undisturbed by corporate and government influence.

3.  Using campaigns and long-term casework to influence human rights concerns using stories of at-risk individuals to the international media.

4.  Hold the attention of government officials, policy makers, corporations, and international institutions.

5.  As advocates, Amnesty promotes legislation and policies to advance human rights by integrating media and grassroots mobilization that assists to protect individuals and free prisoners of conscience.[83]

## FEWER

The Forum of Early Warning and Early Response-Africa (FEWER) has worked in Rwanda, Burundi, and the Democratic Republic of Congo and other African states. FEWER uses an early warning and response system. Four elements of the system help to uncover warning signs: systematic training and capacity building; conflict monitoring, analysis, and reporting; policy response and strategy development; and raising awareness. Training and Capacity Building

---

[82]Amnesty International, "Science for Human Rights," http://www.amnestyusa.org/research/science-for-human-rights (accessed 17 August 2012).

[83]Amnesty International, "About Us: Mission," http://www.amnestyusa.org/about-us/our-mission (accessed 15 August 2012).

relies upon accurate and reliable analysis through training others in the process. The two-step approach focuses first on the partner organizations, to ensure the mechanisms and institutional structures needs are available for the program, and engage with community institutions represented in the analysis--donors and policy makers. The second step of the approach trains on the FEWER Africa conflict analysis methodology.[84]

Their purposes are the following: "Analysis on conflict dynamics for practical use by policy-makers." [85] "Ensure that local, regional and international actors participate in and 'own' conflict prevention and peacebuilding activities."[86] Early warning and response systems focus on systematic training and capacity building, conflict monitoring, analysis, and reporting; policy response and strategy development; an raising awareness.[87]

## FIDH

Federation international des ligue des droits de l'homme (FIDH), translated in English as the International Federation for Human Rights, is a non-partisan, non-religious, apolitical and non-profit organization headquartered in France. FIDH has 164 members from around the world that meet to decide thematic and geographical priorities in human rights based upon equality, dignity and freedom for all human beings. FIDH uses the Universal Declaration of Human Rights (UDHR) as the profile for warning signs and indictors that are viewed, analyzed, and reported. Warning signs and indicators are, therefore, violations of the articles of the Universal Declaration of Human Rights.

---

[84]FEWER, "Early Warning Early Response," http://www fewer-international.org/pages/africa/projects_14.html (accessed 16 August 2012).

[85]FEWER, "FEWER Africa," http://www fewer-international.org/pages/africa/ (accessed 16 August 2012).

[86]Ibid.

[87]FEWER, "Early Warning Early Response."

FIDH's mission to protect and support human rights defenders accomplishes through a joint program called the Observatory for the Protection of Human Rights Defenders with the World Organization Against Torture (OMCT), a program started in 1997. The program supports defenders and their abilities to act. Modes of action include:

> Emergency alerts (urgent appeals, press releases, open or closed letters to the authorities), documentation of violations and an analysis of the causes (international fact-finding missions), direct support (material assistance, relocation, trial observation, defense missions, solidarity missions) and the mobilisation of inter-governmental organisations and public opinion (communications, direct advocacy, campaigns, publication of an annual report).[88]

They defend civil, political, economic and cultural rights, established from the Universal Declaration of Human Rights, acting in legal and political fields for implementation of international instruments to protect human rights and for human rights implementation. A federalist movement acting through national member and partner organizations working with local civil societies to identify local obstacles and mobilize support to overcome them.[89]

## Human Right Watch (HRW)

Human Rights Watch (HRW), an independent, nongovernmental organization, supported by contributions from private individuals and foundations worldwide, accepts no government funds, directly or indirectly. HRW has served for over 30 years, with divisions covering Africa, the Americas, Asia, and the Middle East, North Africa, and a United States program. They have offices globally and 20 field presences outside of their offices. Their methodology investigates 90 countries for human rights abuses. They actively research, report, and advocate change. They choose their focus countries and the issues to address. HRW bases this upon their intuition and

---

[88]FIDH, *Annual Report 2010* (Paris: FIDH, 2010), 12.
[89]Ibid., 4.

experience, and where they believe they can make a positive change. They respond to emergencies; however, they challenge standing or steadily deteriorating human rights problems worldwide.

HRW uses 80 staff researchers. "The researchers work to an established, proven, and consistent methodology based on information gathering from a broad range of sources, and with field-based research at its core."[90] Their purposes are the following:

1.  Defend and protect human rights.

2.  Support the oppressed and hold perpetrators accountable for crimes.

3.  Production of rigorous and objective investigations.

4.  Build strategic and targeted advocacy with intense pressure for action.

5.  Change legal and moral structures for a change for better justice and security for everyone in the world.

6.  Prevent discrimination by supporting victims and activists, uphold political freedom, protect people from inhumane wartime conduct, and to bring justice to perpetrators.

7.  Investigate and expose human rights violations; holding abusers accountable.

8.  Challenge governments and power brokers to end abusive practices and respect international human rights law. [91]

## International Crisis Group (ICG)

The International Crisis Group is an independent, non-profit, non-governmental organization committed to preventing and resolving deadly conflict. Founded in 1995, they have

---

[90]Human Rights Watch, "Methodology," http://www.hrw.org/node/75141 (accessed 10 August 2010).

[91]Human Rights Watch, "About Us," http://www.hrw.org/about (accessed 10 August 2010).

a 150 permanent staff worldwide with 50 nationalities speaking 53 languages. ICG has estimated that 159,000 people subscribing online to receive their reports and over 2 million website visits occur annually. ICG reports on conflict prevention and resolution across the world for issues dealing with Islamist terrorism, nuclear proliferation, local conflict issues, and problems dealing with failed, failing, and fragile states. They have six main roles:

1. Early warning alerts through *CrisisWatch*'s bulletin and specific crisis alerts within the bulletin.

2. Behind the scenes contribution for advice to peace negotiations, with past performance in Sudan, Burundi, Northern Uganda, Zimbabwe.

3. Detailed analysis and advice on policy issues dealing with potential global conflicts. Helping policy makers, UN Security Council, regional organizations, donors, influencers, and at-risk countries to better prevent, manage, and resolve conflict. Also, assisting with rebuilding efforts after conflict.

4. Information on developments on conflict, mass violence and terrorism to policymakers. Examples include Jemash Islamiyah in Indonesia and jihadi groups in Pakistan and Afghanistan.

5. Offer strategic thinking about the world's intractable conflicts to challenge the prevailing ideas.

6. Supporting rules-based vice force-based international order. Influencing UN resolutions and international institutional structures, especially in relation to the norm of the Responsibility to Protect.[92]

---

[92]International Crisis Group, "About Crisis Group," http://www.crisisgroup.org/en/about.aspx (accessed 18 August 2012).

Through 130 staff members on five different continents, Crisis Group uses field-based analysis for high level advocacy to prevent and resolve deadly conflict. They base their approach on field workers located within the countries at risk of outbreak, escalation, or a return to violent conflict. Information and assessments come from the field. They make recommendations to key international decision-makers.

## Genocide Watch

Genocide Watch is the Coordinating organization of The International Alliance to End Genocide (IAEG), an international coalition of organizations. The IAEG educates the general public and policy makers about genocide to create the institutions and political will to prevent and stop genocide, and bring perpetrators to justice. Genocide Watch produces alerts on countries in high-risk conditions and reports monthly on current countries at risk of genocide, politicide, or mass atrocities. Genocide Watch uses a methodology from Dr. Stanton's "Eight Stages of Genocide." Genocide Watch acts as the coordinating agent organization for The International Alliance to End Genocide (IAEG), which is an international coalition of organizations. IAEG educates the public and policy makers about the causes, processes, and warning signs of genocide. They do this to create institutional and political will to prevent and stop genocide and to prosecute perpetrators of genocide.

Genocide Watch has objectives in education, prediction, prevention, intervention, and justice. Education plays the role to raise awareness of specific high-risk situations and genocide as a global issue. Prediction uses models such as Dr. Stanton's "Eight Stages of Genocide" as an instrument to analyze situations for educational, policy analysis, and advocacy purposes. Genocide Watch monitors high-risk areas where genocide is alleged and declare Genocide

Watches, Warnings, and Emergencies. With these declarations come recommendations for options for governments, international organizations, and NGOs to prevent genocide.[93]

Genocide Watch has objectives in education, prediction, prevention, intervention, and justice. Their purpose: "Genocide Watch exists to predict, prevent, stop, and punish genocide and other forms of mass murder. We seek to raise awareness and influence public policy concerning potential and actual genocide. Our purpose is to build an international movement to prevent and stop genocide."[94]

## Harvard Humanitarian Initiative

The Harvard Humanitarian Initiative (HHI), as part of their mission, "promotes evidence-based approaches to humanitarian assistance."[95] HHI, as an academic community, aims to "relieve human suffering in war and disaster by advancing the science and practice of humanitarian response worldwide."[96] It conducts studies about high-risk areas that involve discovering the indicators and of violence occurring or maturing. The studies follow clear methodologies and offer a scientific approach to the problems, discussions, and recommendations. The same methodologies could possibly be used by other researchers as generalizable, and offer the same results in different high-risk areas; therefore, they are important in information and techniques to R2P and GMA early warning and indicators.

For example, HHI released its collaborative study on the LRA's effects upon the civilian population within the Democratic Republic of Congo (DRC) using HHI academic approach with

---

[93]Genocide Watch, "About Us," http://www.genocidewatch.org/aboutus/missionstatement html (accessed 18 August 2012).

[94]Ibid.

[95]Harvard Humanitarian Initiative, "Harvard Humanitarian Initiative," http://www.hhi.harvard.edu/ (accessed 17 July 2012).

[96]Ibid.

the international organization called Discover the Journey (DTJ) to document the effects. They

drew accounts from those affected, and currently affected, "including former LRA abductees and

their families, as well as community leaders, women's groups representatives, and local and

international organizations."[97] The methodology followed:

> Thirty-three semi-structured qualitative interviews conducted in four communities in
> northeastern Democratic Republic of Congo (DRC) that are highly exposed to LRA
> violence. The research instrument was created based on informational interviews with
> NGO staff and community members in affected areas, and refined after pilot interviews
> in Dungu.[98]

The aforementioned report indicated significant results from a useful context by applied

qualitative studies with a relevant survey population. The results indicated logical identification

of the problems for the communities affected by the violence of the LRA and suggest prevention

and resiliency techniques based upon the data and information researched. As this was academic

research, the validation techniques used were consistent, documented, conformed to the

Institution Review Board (IRB) standards. The coding methods used with researchers later were

entered into a database to draw relationships between categories.[99] Analysis and

recommendations flowed from the research, enabling contextualized solutions and insight into the

on-going crisis.

Third party and academic methodologies into early warning signs, interviews, and

participation provide useful ways for organizing effort to observe and identify early warning

signs and indicators.

---

[97]Lindsay Branham and Jocelyn Kelly, *We Suffer From War and More War: Assessment Of The Impact Of The Lord's Resistance Army On Formerly Abducted Children and Their CommunitiesIn Northeastern Democratic Republic Of The Congo* (DTJ Publications, 2012), 10.

[98]Ibid.

[99]Ibid., 17.

# Section 4: Analysis

An important assumption made in genocide and mass atrocity early warning and indicators is that the early warning can prevent GMA. Conflict resolution also works in the same manner. Genocide and atrocity most often occur during war or conflict. The warning signs and indicators of conflict and war, therefore, provide useful tools for indicators or scenarios involving mass atrocity and genocide and for signaling discourse about obligations under the signed provisions in the Responsibility to Protect. Third party methodologies observed and used these assumptions. If one averts war and conflict, it assumes, one deters genocide and mass atrocity. A planner may therefore use these early warning signs and indicators to understand the context of current affairs, probability of conflict, and likelihood of GMA to occur.

Another caveat offered by the Secretary-General of the U.N. states that conflict may not be the only indicator of mass atrocity and genocide. In fact, other sources of instability offer alternative assumptions about what indictors and warning signs might lead a situation into mass atrocity and genocide. This research concludes that third parties offer useful early warning and indicators in three respects: as a methodology for observations, to identify the common early warning indicators used, and as methodologies that bring out warning and indicators which predict or have a purpose in their usefulness as indicators.

Several researched methodologies contain core ideas or values based upon the assumption of curbing violence, war, conflict, human rights violations, and more generally, a system to enforce or observe violations of human rights, or allegations. Third parties adopted a general framework or model to support their methodologies. The Sentinel Satellite Project (SSP) and UNOSAT use the idea of possible threats to human security and human rights.[100] WITNESS

uses video to expose these abuses in real-time. The baseline framework for the International

Crisis Group relies upon deadly conflict[101] and is similar to FEWER's response to violent

conflict.[102] Human Rights Watch focuses on violations of human rights and human rights

abuses.[103] FIDH's baseline defends the Universal Declaration of Human Rights,[104] along with

Amnesty International.[105] The UN, Special Advisor on the Prevention of Genocide's framework

involves "massive and serious violations of human rights and international humanitarian law of

ethnic and racial origin that, if not prevented or halted, might lead to genocide".[106]

The methodology used by third parties assists with observing conditions leading to mass

atrocity and genocide. The framework distinguishes the signals and information requiring

observation. The signals and vantage points chosen for observation, like an experiment, require

reliability and validation of the observed facts. The information compares with violations of

human rights laws, possible and actual violence, and the potential of genocide and mass atrocity

stemming from the conditions. Therefore, the framework determines the early warning signs or

the indicators of human rights abuses that signal the possibilities of instability, conflict, genocide,

and mass atrocity. These are uniquely useful in R2P by themselves because predicting violent

---

[100]Satellite Sentinel Project, "Our Story," http://satsentinel.org/our-story (accessed 3 August, 2012); United Nations Institute for Training and Research, "Satellite Applications for Human Security," UNOSAT Brief, Washington, DC, 2011, 9.

[101]International Crisis Group, Asia Report No. 204, *Tajinkistan: The Changing Insurgent Threats* (Washington, DC: International Crisis Group, 2011), 21.

[102]FEWER. "FEWER Africa."

[103]Human Rights Watch, "About Us," http://www.hrw.org/about (accessed 10 August 2010).

[104]FIDH, *Annual Report 2010,* 4.

[105]Amnesty International.

[106]Office of the Special Adviser on the Prevention of Genocide.

conflict includes many variables, root causes, complexities of interaction, conflict models, and accuracy of information that analysis and decision-making rely heavily upon to make the most appropriate and applicable choices.[107]

These third parties see themselves as researchers or investigators. Consistent with this view, they pursue ways of investigating and observing human rights violations with reliable standards. Internal policies and practices also help ensure accuracy and provide legitimate indicators and warnings to their work. Consequently, third parties see their reputations as a method and motivation for accuracy. Maintaining trust in reporting serves their stakeholders (donors, civil society, minorities, employees, grass-root supporters, etc.) and forms an important and validating relationship between the two. As subject matter experts in their field of expertise, they are relied upon for specific information in high human risk environments, also useful to R2P because early warning aides states' accountability through useful context and information that corresponds to developing systems of international justice.[108] This is important to policy-makers and crisis planners because the information is unique and close to the situation.

Collection techniques offer clues about the accuracy and reliability of third party information. The U.N. Special Advisor to Genocide relied upon collection of information from their existing systems such as the UNOSAT.[109] UNOSAT partnered with the European Organization for Nuclear Research (CERN) to establish reliable methods for their conflict mapping and tracking systems and Amnesty International maintains a program called Science in

---

[107]International Commission on Intervention and State Sovereignty, 21.

[108]General Assembly Security Council United Nations, 6.

[109]Office of the Special Adviser on the Prevention of Genocide.

Human Rights using technological advances in science for their reliability. [110][111] The Sentinel Satellite Project teamed up with the Harvard Humanitarian Initiative (HHI) to form a reliable methodology for satellite imagery research. The International Crisis Group uses field-based staff in 130 countries to provide analysis for high-level advocacy. They rely upon not only their fieldwork, but on their reports, and the integrity of the organization's co-chairmanship with former European Commission for External Relations and a former U.S. ambassador. The reputation of their *CrisisWatch* bulletin informs their accuracy and trust they have with their stakeholders who continue to rely upon their analysis. Human Rights Watch calls their team "staff researchers" and use a broad range of sources for information and field-based research as the core of their reliability to their methodology. [112] FEWER used systematic training in capacity building for accurate and reliable ways to deliver analysis on the early warning and response systems used. [113]

As researchers to observable human conditions, each of the third parties pursued a methodology to monitor, provide analysis, and report upon early warning signs and indicators. Accuracy and reliability were important parameters within methodologies. Both direct and indirect methods were used together. Direct contact observation monitors in real-time by being present at human events. Indirect methods use observation separated from direct contact with the event. For example, a technological device (camera, satellite imagery, unmanned aerial aircraft) or witness interview provides useful information about past events. Often a combination of these methods corroborated the results of monitoring and reporting. Further analysis of the

---

[110]United Nations Institute for Training and Research, *AT Brief: Satellite Applications for Human Security*, (Washington, DC: UNITAR, 2011), 9.

[111]Amnesty International.

[112]Human Rights Watch.

[113]FEWER, "Early Warning Early Response."

corroborated data and information allows development of a true picture of the situation with the goal to reporting accuracy.

The output of third party organizations serves as useful to the MAPRO lens because these regional and sub-regional organizations will be critical in GMA prevention because of their direct interest. They also can be key players and influencers in the UN and the U.S. can use their output to gain support and advocacy to U.S. policies and programs to amplify efforts.[114]

Third parties answer critical information requirements and gaps that the MAPRO finds to be key areas of information relating to the GMA situation. Potentially, third parties fill in information related to perpetrators, their supporters, and other adversaries or people of interest. Third parties can identify the victim groups, those presenting positive action, and those who might be able to intervene. Additionally, information is also provided about the specifics of violence against civilians, and the reactions of the host nation government to these incidents. Third parties can offer the context about nations' attitudes, policy changes, and composition as they relate to violence and GMA situations.[115]

Third parties offer an outside perspective to the challenges and issues that implementing partners in conflict and stability are having with their programs. This information can be useful to understand if the actions used are offering the calculated results and perhaps move toward more effective action. In addition, third parties can assist with understanding what other resources or solutions might exist at the regional level that were not thought of by those outside the first-hand situation or offer alternative solutions.[116]

---

[114]U.S. Army Peacekeeping and Stability Operations Institute, 87.

[115]Ibid., 51.

[116]Ibid.

Military operational planners can use third party information to their advantage because the military does not look for the early warning signs and indicators and does not have mechanisms to do so. This information becomes useful in opening up other options and solutions that likely were not acknowledged. The information, often found by open source avenues, provides relevant and critical information about the context of conflict or possible GMA situations that could lead to conflict. Although some third parties may want to remain outside of the interest of governments to retain their neutrality, their information may still be accessed in the open source networks, verified for accuracy, and used by policy-makers and planners.

The MAPRO speaks of third party actors as partners with the U.S. in GMA situations; however, the research uncovered that critical information may be obtained from third parties that will never partner directly with the U.S. or other governments. Access to third party information via the web or open sources provides access to the critical GMA information that is reliable and useful for MAPRO purposes.

Another topic of discussion involved social media and the rapid dispersion of innovation and ideas that social media offers in GMA situations. Academic interdisciplinary collaboration in GMA warning signs and indicators offers important methods and information to existing social media. Vetting information on 13 June 2009, during the Iranian protests of the national elections, was essential because "misinformation gained currency simply by being constantly repeated or re-tweeted."[117] This was an event indicator of the difficulties of the new technology (social media) and information sharing during crisis and emergencies.[118] Organized communities require objective and accurate information, a 'public good', especially during crisis when critical

---

[117]Diane Coyle and Patrick Meier, *New Technologies in Emergencies and Conflicts: The Role of Information and Social Networks* (Washington, DC: UN Foundation-Vodafone Foundation Partnership, 2009), 3.

[118]Ibid.

information helps in response.[119] Assisting with the use of technologies to improve, prepare, respond, and recover from disasters and conflict has risks, challenges, and demands a balance with rapid access and reliable information for communities to maintain resilience or assistance.[120] Accordingly, people in crisis benefit from accurate information flow and "if communities depend on information for their survival in times of crisis, then communication technologies are their lifelines."[121]

Information Communications Technology (ICT) seems to offer assistance to the identification of conflict and possible GMA indicators when they exist. Patrick Meier and Jennifer Leaning believed that ICTs used in "conflict early warning, crisis mapping and humanitarian response" were changing and offered significance to conflict warnings.[122] ICTs plays three important roles: "facilitating the communications of information in conflict zones, improving the collection of salient quantitative and qualitative conflict data, and enhancing the visualization and analysis of patterns."[123]

ICTs provide useful information to GMA situations and conflicts when the data uses reliability methods ensuring accuracy. Many academic and third party organizations, such as Harvard Humanitarian Initiative and WITNESS, use ways of fact-checking information by triangulating sources with communications technology linked with global positioning systems with reliable witness accounts. This information is not only critical to crisis planning but affords alerts, survival, and opportunity for possible victims of GMA or conflict.

---

[119]Ibid.

[120]Ibid.

[121]Ibid., 4.

[122]Patrick Meier and Jennifer Leaning, *Applying Technology to Crisis Mapping and Early Warning in Humanitarian Settings* (Cambridge, MA: Harvard Humanitarian Initiative, 2009), 2.

[123]Ibid.

## Observed Warning Signs

The common warning signs observed derived mainly from the United Nations Special Advisor on the Prevention of Genocide (See Appendix D, OSAPG Analysis). The first seven factors of the analysis framework deal mainly with historical risk data and information—mainly comparisons of genocidal risk situations currently residing within a state, that through analysis of the factors provide a scale of likelihood of mass atrocity and genocide. The eighth factor in the Analysis Framework, however, predicts future events (events on the horizon that have not occurred, but are a general tendency of governments) that might trigger instability or conflict that would lead to genocide or mass atrocity. Each of the international organizations was informed by the United Nations Special Advisor on the Prevention of Genocide Analysis Framework.

Third parties that used technological advances to identify warning signs looked for evidence of pending mass violence using a forensic type analysis linked to a logical narrative of events that occurred from the past. Additionally, third parties offered prediction of danger or possible imminent high-risk situations from previously gathered analysis and data formulated from a specific region or area. The methodologies supported useful indicators to past genocide and mass atrocity; whereby allowing historic data to assist in forming predictive analysis for future GMA events. Moreover, predictions about imminent threats to civilians drew upon the trends generated from past data and analysis and a narrative explaining the events or the predictions in published works on the internet or reported in the mass media. These sources are highly useful to the U.S. obligation in the R2P and valuable to policy-makers and their planners.

A common early warning theme for international organizations were signs in the areas of humanitarian affairs and relief coordination, monitoring, capacity development, and technical assistance. Warning signs were used for mapping crisis and current situations, for assessing the damage and impact to populations, and for monitoring the human security or risks. The monitoring function looked at the systems in place to verify safety and human security, observe human rights violations or compliance, and continue to view and examine territorial planning. Warning signs established surveillance on country projects and development and the implementation of those projects--to check their progress and assess the results. Alerts to civilians gave warning and survival information to civilians who might become victims. Warnings to possible perpetrators put them on alert to their possible GMA actions, and quite possibly may prevent them from the actions.

While all third parties viewed human rights abuses, warning signs, and indicators of abuse, not all specifically reported them using video. Warning signs captured on video are useful to alert and give evidence to situations possibly moving toward genocide and mass atrocity. The use of video acted as a survey instrument first, as a method of capturing interviews and recording testimony or witness accounts. As an instrument of a survey, video acted as a credible and accurate source, while footage provided multiple purposes. Video with equal voice and impartiality to both sides of an issue, encompassed a more holistic understanding of the human rights abuses and a valuable tool for providing context. Video footage and documentation offers vivid and compelling indicators and warnings to mass atrocity and genocide, and sometimes adds those resources through social media, allowing for the dispersion of critical information valuable to crisis planners and potential victims.

The Universal Declaration of Human Rights (UDHR) offered a framework for "what" to observe. International organizations used the UDHR as a basis to report on violations when they occurred. The UDHR provided the outline for fact-finding missions for countries in transition, encountering new elections, or possibly moving towards resuming conflict. Other international organizations, instead of looking for violations, observed conflict and peace generating factors, root and proximate causes, conflict triggers, indicators of peace, stakeholder interests, agendas, and capacities. Each of these viewpoints warns of instability leading to genocide and mass atrocity. These are useful for military planners concerned about future threats, force capabilities, and the tools and options to deal with pending conflict.

Early warning dealing with conflict prevention and resolution dealt mainly with terrorism, nuclear proliferation, local conflict issues, and the problems for failed, fragile, and failing states or a theme of deterioration of the following factors: peace, justice, gender, climate change, and the responsibility to protect. These are issues relevant to policy-makers and planners trying to meet requirements of the R2P while also preventing or stopping GMA.

Lastly, Genocide Watch used Dr. Stanton's "8 Stages of Genocide" as a prediction instrument to code analysis of at-risk countries and signal warnings of genocide.[124] Genocide Watch's warning signs alert to high-risk States. The "8 Stages" method analyzes the situation each month and constitutes a data base of analysis that gives snapshots over time to allow for further analysis, action, prediction, and context to scenarios possibly moving toward mass atrocity.

**Purpose of Warning Signs and Indicators**

The singular purpose for generating warning signs and indicators is to prevent mass atrocity and genocide by documenting abuses and violations of human rights and to bring the issues to an authority for policy action. Raising awareness, alerting, and advocacy are the three main objectives for reporting and looking for warning signs and indicators.

Third parties monitoring mass atrocity and genocide in high-risk conditions provide uniquely useful indicators/warnings of possible mass atrocity and genocide. These activities can be critical to U.S. efforts to meet its obligations under the Responsibility to Protect (R2P). The foremost imperatives for preventing genocide and mass atrocity require a "reliable process for

---

[124]Genocide Watch.

assessing risks and generating early warning of potential atrocities" which third parties provide.[125] Academic institutions have tested and reliable methodologies into early warning signs, interviews, and participation which provides useful ways for organizing efforts to observe and identify early warning signs and indicators.

Early warning signs and indicators act as both alerting mechanisms as well as a mechanism for prevention. The duality anticipates the causes of instability and the stages of genocide and mass atrocity while at the same time offering an assessment of the situation alerting and implementing the prevention to the impending dangers. Sometimes it is difficult to understand where early warning and prevention begin and end; especially when the warning signs are historic indicators that have often triggered mass atrocity and genocide. War and conflict in most cases, indicate the imminent possibility of genocide and mass atrocity. Understanding the warning signs to conflict, provides the ready answers to prevention.

In the event of conflict, the monitoring and prevention efforts have already been established and provide assistance to bringing the violence down, indicating and validating claims, and helping in the stability efforts when the conflict subsides. The Council on Foreign Relations Special Report Number 62 offers the preventive areas as effective in pre-conflict preventive measures, which also serves as good basic measures and techniques before violence erupts: Electoral processes/political transitions; Ethnic/religious frictions; Boundary/territorial disputes; Resource/food scarcities; and Special investigations.[126] (See Appendix E, Indicators and Prevention) Each of these preventative measures assists in addressing the problems of violence and instability through early warning, monitoring, and prevention. Special investigations assist in

---

[125]Madeline K. Albright and William S. Cohen, *Preventing Genocide: A Blueprint for U.S. Policymakers* (Washington, DC: United States Holocaust Memorial Museum, The American Academy of Diplocacy, and the Endowment of the United States Institute of Peace, 2008), 17.

[126]Stares and Zenko, 8-11.

the process of validating claims of human rights abuses or violations of international law, while also acting as an early warning and preventative measure.

> Should earlier preventive efforts fail to have the desired effect or violence erupt with little or no warning, many of the same basic measures and techniques can be employed to manage and mitigate the crisis. These include efforts targeted at the parties to a conflict to facilitate cooperative dispute resolution and change their incentive structures to promote peaceful outcomes.[127]

Additionally, the key to warning signs is to find balance in the instability with measures or prevention to stabilize them. Early warning indicators, in the general sense, are at our feet right now because we understand the trends related to instability leading to conflict and war and ultimately genocide and mass atrocity. What we have in details now are from a long view or longitudinal analysis and are still on-going.

The reality is that conflict flares up in an instant, a human phenomenon. Early warning signs purposefully alert us to the first signs of imminent genocide and mass atrocity giving context and reporting to the situation. It never ceases, whether in peace and stability, or war and instability. To warn early and to prevent are inseparable in their implementation. Plans made that offer techniques to prevent genocide and mass atrocity are the same plans for systems and mechanism that need to be in place when instability occurs. By monitoring and assessing the situation you can prudently react and respond accordingly.

The most important aspects of warning signs are accuracy and reliability. This allows the information to function in support of decision-making. The constant throughout the decision-making process or conflict cycle (in either short or long term decision making) relies upon context, understanding, visualizing, and describing, so as to direct the and assess the situations

---

[127]Ibid., 11.

48

further. Third party methodologies are uniquely useful in the steps required to form a true picture of the situation in its context; allowing for proper and relevant decision-making.

Additionally, governments or more accurately their policy-makers are the core audience for third parties to influence stakeholders to follow the Universal Declaration of Human Rights and the Responsibility to Protect. Third parties inform their interests and audience with relevant, accurate, and reliable information that governments find useful because the information has been gathered, analyzed, synthesized, and presented as knowledge and understanding. This assists governments to decide by addressing the problems and complexities of the situations, the obstacles leading to a peaceful and stable resolution to conflict and instability potentially leading to GMA.

Early intervention to prevent crisis has not been the strength of third parties because of drawing consensus for collective action, different interests of the member states, different opinions about assessments, and warning signs leading to violent conflict. Quiet diplomacy or discreet diplomatic strategies have been used as preventive measures because they can bypass, in some sense, the collaboration required to prevent conflict; and because normally, stabilization and reconstruction efforts after conflict have become so much of an issue.[128] Early warning signs assist in looking beyond and after conflict and provide the basis for continued or sustainable stability. Early warning does not just offer prevention to conflict and instability, but provides options for peaceful options.

Early warning signs picked up by third parties are often refuted by governments alleged to have committed violations of human rights. At times, governments try to stop third parties from monitoring, preventing them from reporting to the international community, or censoring

---

[128]Ibid., 9.

their data. These are indicators of the indicators. In essence, these are additional red flags that alert government cover-ups and human rights violations. Third parties provide these useful indicators. The types of political prisoners and the reasons for wrongful detention give practical information about allegations or tendencies of governments to lose sight of their responsibility to protect.

## Section 5: Conclusions and Recommendations

Third parties are effective in their efforts to provide early warnings and indicators of possible mass atrocity and genocide events because their methodologies are reliable, verifiable, monitored legitimate warning signs and indicators, and contained purposefulness in documentation and prevention. Third parties implement most of the risk-reducing actions at the regional levels establishing the "basic rules and norms of responsible state behavior."[129]

Each third party uses acceptable frameworks to observe and report human rights violations. These frameworks assist with identifying what to observe. Some examples include, the Universal Declaration of Human Rights, human security issues, human rights abuses, deadly and violent conflict, violations of or deficiencies in humanitarian law, and scenarios of likely cultural or social instability. Early warning signs and indicators contain reliability and validation of facts and observations that seek the signs of conflict/instability leading to genocide and mass atrocity. Because third parties observe from the "researchers" and "investigators" viewpoint, the evidence collected becomes empirical evidence with broad use as facts bearing on the GMA situation. In some cases, the field work used interviews following the acceptable measures and procedures of

---

[129]Ibid., 7.

the Institution Review Board. HHI, FIDH, and HRW offer the best practices and methods for participant interviewing.

Another way to effectively provide early warning indicators and analysis came through a sense of organizational reputation. This was a mechanism for providing accurate, credible, and legitimate information to stakeholders and ensuring managerial and institutional oversight of collection and reporting. Active partnerships with other reliable actors making use of sound methodologies, techniques, practices, mutual oversight, and verification also assisted in providing facts. Corroboration of events and sources assisted in reporting accuracy. Properly resourced publications with reliable resources and human sources, along with fact-finding functions proximate with events, gave reliable context to actual events. Third parties were transparent in their methodologies which had generalizability as best practices for others' use. International Crisis Group and Genocide Watch offer reliable methods that policy-makers and planners can use in their own work.

More valuable information about early warning can be gained from third parties because their methods assure timely and accurate information, uncensored by governments, because they have accessibility to high-risk events. This helps to allow information to be released that would otherwise be censored or prevented from release and gives insight into potential GMA or conflict events. Third parties were viewed as experts in the field of prevention of mass atrocity and genocide with the capacity and willingness to provide and identify limitations on the early warning signs and indicators reported. Overall, they seek and report the truth, corroborate for veracity, protect the security and dignity of witnesses, and remain impartial.

Early warning naturally scans and identifies possible conflict generating scenarios because genocide most often forms in the context of violence. Therefore, actions mitigating conflict "have a direct and positive impact on preventing genocide and mass atrocity."[130] To combine early warning or bridge the gap between alerting and preventing, "early prevention requires a multifaceted strategy that simultaneously reduces capacities and motivations for mass violence while increasing the social and institutional safeguards against mass violence."[131] Early warning tools need to be in place to deliver the performance and effectiveness of conflict resolution. This gives evidentially based reporting with a mechanism to measure effective prevention strategy.

Governments and the military have difficulty in high-risk settings identifying indicators of mass atrocity and genocide by themselves. Collaboration and coordination of effort between these actors can not only save time, but help to validate claims. Additionally, a methodology for discovering and mapping complexity, understanding the operational environment, the desired end-state, and the right problem in relation to the current information is a gap in MAPRO. MAPRO presents a decision-making process; however, there is usefulness in a methodology to understand the complexities of the situation before pushing a decision to a higher level policy-maker. A recommendation is for the use of the Army Design Methodology to assess possible scenarios of mass atrocity and genocide.

U.S. Army Design Methodology "[applies] critical and creative thinking to understand, visualize, and describe unfamiliar problems and approaches to solving them."[132] The methodology, iterative in nature, assists to form an operational approach to solve problems. Some of the important outputs of the methodology bring about an environmental frame, problem

---

[130]Albright and Cohen, *Preventing Genocide*, 38.

[131]Ibid., 41.

[132]Headquarters, Department of the Army, Field Manual (FM) 5-0, *Army Doctrine Publication* (Washington, DC: Government Printing Office, 2010), 7.

frames, improved understanding, and an "operational approach that serves as the link between conceptual and detailed planning."[133] Therefore, if the information obtained from third parties provides effective warning signs and indicators of mass atrocity and genocide, then using Army Design Methodology assists with and allows understanding, visualizing, and describing the situation in its proper frame and narrative. Furthermore, proper context allows decision-makers to make informed decisions supporting obligations of R2P and increasing efforts to prevent mass atrocity and genocide through planned action tailored to meet the future crisis.

Another recommendation follows to capture the importance of collaboration and streamlining information. Collaboration has many useful benefits from gaining holistic, complex, and contextualized information. On the other hand, there is difficulty facilitating all of the various international and other organizations concerned with early warning on GMA, to form a unity of effort. The recommendation is to institutionalize a body of trained strategists and planners, able to use a methodology, much like the Army Design Methodology, to bring understanding to the huge amounts of information and complexity, and then carry out a decision-making process such as the MAPRO to offer solutions with planning details and actions relevant to the situation; ultimately, meeting the demand to stop GMA.

Streamlining humanitarian efforts helps to share the burdens and also bring about a greater unity of effort to identify early warning indicators of mass atrocity and genocide. FIDH found that another organization monitored the conflict problem in Democratic Republic of Congo (DRC) effectively, and therefore, they shifted their efforts to fight for policy against impunity for perpetrators of serious crimes. The shift in effort showed that they were not producing a

---

[133]Ibid.

redundant and unnecessary effort, but could, however, expand upon another early warning indicator in human rights advocacy. This is a benefit to collaboration and information sharing.

The last recommendation involves information sharing. Most third parties were clear on their methodologies used for early warning; however, some were not. When reporting it is valuable to register how information was obtained. In instances where disclosure would compromise the observer or the observation, then the only recourse is to indicate a reputable source. This can only be accomplished from long standing organizations with excellent reputations, or undeniably accurate and credible information such as videos or testimonies. A planner or decision-maker could find credible information from some of the relevant GMA "clearinghouses" such as Genocide Watch, International Crisis Group, and FEWER-Africa and compare their assessments then corroborate that information with the facts or information already available on the GMA situation in question.

# APPENDIX A

# 8 Stages of Genocide

By Gregory H. Stanton, President, Genocide Watch

Classification Symbolization Dehumanization Organization Polarization Preparation Extermination Denial

Genocide is a process that develops in eight stages that are predictable but not inexorable. At each stage, preventive measures can stop it. The process is not linear. Logically, later stages must be preceded by earlier stages. But all stages continue to operate throughout the process.

http://www.genocidewatch.org/aboutgenocide/8stagesofgenocide.html

Accessed on 27 JUN 2012

| Stages | Description |
|---|---|
| 1. CLASSIFICATION | All cultures have categories to distinguish people into "us and them" by ethnicity, race, religion, or nationality: German and Jew, Hutu and Tutsi. Bipolar societies that lack mixed categories, such as Rwanda and Burundi, are the most likely to have genocide. The main preventive measure at this early stage is to develop universalistic institutions that transcend ethnic or racial divisions, that actively promote tolerance and understanding, and that promote classifications that transcend the divisions. The Catholic church could have played this role in Rwanda, had it not been riven by the same ethnic cleavages as Rwandan society. Promotion of a common language in countries like Tanzania has also promoted transcendent national identity. This search for common ground is vital to early prevention of genocide. |
| 2. SYMBOLIZATION | We give names or other symbols to the classifications. We name people "Jews" or "Gypsies", or distinguish them by colors or dress; and apply the symbols to members of groups. Classification and symbolization are universally human and do not necessarily result in genocide unless they lead to the next stage, dehumanization. When combined with hatred, symbols may be forced upon unwilling members of pariah groups: the yellow star for Jews under Nazi rule, the blue scarf for people from the Eastern Zone in Khmer Rouge Cambodia. To combat symbolization, hate symbols can be legally forbidden (swastikas) as can hate speech. Group marking like gang clothing or tribal scarring can be outlawed, as well. The problem is that legal limitations will fail if unsupported by popular cultural enforcement. Though Hutu and Tutsi were forbidden words in Burundi until the 1980's, code-words replaced them. If widely supported, however, denial of symbolization can be powerful, as it was in Bulgaria, where the government refused to supply enough yellow badges and at least eighty percent of Jews did not wear them, depriving the yellow star of its significance as a Nazi symbol for Jews. |
| 3. DEHUMANIZATION | One group denies the humanity of the other group. Members of it are equated with animals, vermin, insects or diseases. Dehumanization overcomes the normal human revulsion against murder. At this stage, hate propaganda in print and on hate radios is used to vilify the victim group. In combating this dehumanization, incitement to genocide should not be confused with protected speech. Genocidal societies lack constitutional protection for countervailing speech, and should be treated differently than democracies. Local and international leaders should condemn the use of hate speech and make it culturally unacceptable. Leaders who incite genocide should be banned from international travel and have their foreign finances frozen. Hate radio stations should be shut down, and hate propaganda banned. Hate crimes and atrocities should be promptly punished. |
| 4. ORGANIZATION | Genocide is always organized, usually by the state, often using militias to provide deniability of state responsibility (the Janjaweed in Darfur.) Sometimes organization is informal (Hindu mobs led by local RSS militants) or decentralized (terrorist groups.) Special army units or militias are often trained and armed. Plans are made for genocidal killings. To combat this stage, membership in these militias should be outlawed. Their leaders should be denied visas for foreign travel. The U.N. should impose arms embargoes on governments and citizens of countries involved in genocidal massacres, and create commissions to investigate violations, as was done in post-genocide Rwanda. |
| 5. POLARIZATION | Extremists drive the groups apart. Hate groups broadcast polarizing propaganda. Laws may forbid intermarriage or social interaction. Extremist terrorism targets moderates, intimidating and silencing the center. Moderates from the perpetrators' own group are most able to stop genocide, so are the first to be arrested and killed. Prevention may mean security protection for moderate leaders or assistance to human rights groups. Assets of extremists may be seized, and visas for international travel denied to them. Coups d'état by extremists should be opposed by international sanctions. |
| 6. PREPARATION | Victims are identified and separated out because of their ethnic or religious identity. Death lists are drawn up. Members of victim groups are forced to wear identifying symbols. Their property is expropriated. They are often segregated into ghettoes, deported into concentration camps, or confined to a famine-struck region and starved. At this stage, a Genocide Emergency must be declared. If the political will of the great powers, regional alliances, or the U.N. Security Council can be mobilized, armed international intervention should be prepared, or heavy assistance provided to the victim group to prepare for its self-defense. Otherwise, at least humanitarian assistance should be organized by the U.N. and private relief groups for the inevitable tide of refugees to come. |
| 7. EXTERMINATION | begins, and quickly becomes the mass killing legally called "genocide." It is "extermination" to the killers because they do not believe their victims to be fully human. When it is sponsored by the state, the armed forces often work with militias to do the killing. Sometimes the genocide results in revenge killings by groups against each other, creating the downward whirlpool-like cycle of bilateral genocide (as in Burundi). At this stage, only rapid and overwhelming armed intervention can stop genocide. Real safe areas or refugee escape corridors should be established with heavily armed international protection. (An unsafe "safe" area is worse than none at all.) The U.N. Standing High Readiness Brigade, EU Rapid Response Force, or regional forces -- should be authorized to act by the U.N. Security Council if the genocide is small. For larger interventions, a multilateral force authorized by the U.N. should intervene. If the U.N. is paralyzed, regional alliances must act. It is time to recognize that the international responsibility to protect transcends the narrow interests of individual nation states. If strong nations will not provide troops to intervene directly, they should provide the airlift, equipment, and financial means necessary for regional states to intervene. |
| 8. DENIAL | is the eighth stage that always follows a genocide. It is among the surest indicators of further genocidal massacres. The perpetrators of genocide dig up the mass graves, burn the bodies, try to cover up the evidence and intimidate the witnesses. They deny that they committed any crimes, and often blame what happened on the victims. They block investigations of the crimes, and continue to govern until driven from power by force, when they flee into exile. There they remain with impunity, like Pol Pot or Idi Amin, unless they are captured and a tribunal is established to try them. The response to denial is punishment by an international tribunal or national courts. There the evidence can be heard, and the perpetrators punished. Tribunals like the Yugoslav or Rwanda Tribunals, or an international tribunal to try the Khmer Rouge in Cambodia, or an International Criminal Court may not deter the worst genocidal killers. But with the political will to arrest and prosecute them, some may be brought to justice. |

By Gregory H. Stanton, President, Genocide Watch
Was Presented to the State Department in Organization Preparation Prevention Denial
Classification Symbolization Dehumanization Organization Polarization Preparation Extermination Denial
http://www.genocidewatch.org/aboutgenocide/8stagesofgenocide.html
Accessed on 27 JUN 2012

# APPENDIX B
## The Context of War

| Episode[134] | Perpetrator Centre | Principle Perpetrator Organs | Constitutive War (or history/ threat of war)[135] | Organized armed enemies (or perceived enemies)[136] | Enemy Social Groups |
|---|---|---|---|---|---|
| Armenian genocide, 1915(I) | Ottoman state | Army, police, paramilitaries | WWI | Russia, Britain, France | Armenians |
| Stalin's liquidation of kulaks, 1929-32 (II) | Soviet state | Army, police, party | *Civil war 1919-21 'imperialist' threat* | *Imperialism, counter-revolution* | Peasants, Ukrainians |
| Nazi euthanasia of mentally handicapped, 1930s (III) | Nazi state | Police, party | WWI | *International Jewry, Bolshevism* | Mentally handicapped |
| Rape of Nanking (etc.) 1937 (IV) | Imperial Japanese state | Army | Conquest of China | Chinese government, Communists | Chinese |
| German occupation of Poland, 1939-40 (III) | Nazi state | Army, police, party | Invasion of Poland | Poland, Britain, France | Poles, especially Jews |
| First phase, Holocaust, 1941-2 (III) | Nazi state | Army, police, camp administration | Later stages WWII | USSR and Allies | Jews, Gypsies, etc. |
| Second phase, Holocaust 1942-5 (III) | Nazi state | Army, police, camp administration | Later stages WWII | USSR and Allies | Jews, Gypsies,ect |
| Stalin's deportation of nationalities, 1941-2 (II) | Soviet state | Army, police | WWII | Nazi Germany | Volga Germans, Chechens, etc. |
| "Great Leap Forward", 1959-61 | Chinese state | Army, police, party | *Conflict with USA; Sino-Soviet split* | *USA, USSR* | peasants |
| Massacres of Indonesian Communists, 1965 | Indonesian state (army) | Army, police | *conflict with Malaya* | Indonesian Communist Party | Communists, Chinese |
| Occupation of East Timor, 1975-99 | Indonesian state | Army, police | conquest and counter-insurgency | East Timorese resistance (FRETILIN) | East Timorese |
| Cambodian genocide, 1977-9(VII) | Khmer Rouge state | Party, army | wars with USA, Vietnam | USA, Vietnam | Urban-educated, peasants, Vietnamese minorities |
| Yugoslav wars, 1991-9 (VIII) | Serbian-Yugoslav state + Serbian statelets in Bosnia, Croatia | Parties, armies, police, paramilitaries | Yugoslav wars | Slovenia, Croatia, Bosnia, Kosovo, Liberation Army, NATO | Croats, Muslims, Albanians, plural urban Bosnians |
| Rwandan genocide, 1994 IX) | Rwandan state (ruling party) | Police, militia, armed gangs | Rwandan civil war | Rwandan Patriotic Front (RPF) | Tutsis, opposition parties |

[134]In this column, roman numerals refer to the episode sections of this book.

[135]In this column, italics are used for genocides that did not take place in an immediate context of war as such, but where earlier wars or threats of war provided important elements of context.

[136]In this column, italics are used where 'enemies' were defined ideologically, but where war was not actually taking place.

# APPENDIX C
## Third Party Methodologies Researched

The methodologies of the international organizations researched follow to give an understanding of their practices. The proper starting point is the United Nations Special Adviser on the Prevention of Genocide, which generates the definitions of genocide and mass atrocity, their human rights programs, and the Responsibility to Protect. The U.N. takes the lead on methodologies and analysis frameworks; however, they are obviously not the only implementing third party for early warning and indicators of conflict, instability, genocide, and mass atrocity.

**United Nations**

The United Nations Special Adviser on the Prevention of Genocide uses a clear methodology that forms within the responsibilities of the office. The UN Special Adviser on the Prevention of Genocide (OSAPG) methodology is the standard for early warning of genocide and mass atrocity. The responsibilities of the Special Adviser on the Prevention of Genocide are the following:

"1. Collecting existing information, in particular from within the United Nations system, on massive and serious violations of human rights and international humanitarian law of ethnic and racial origin that, if not prevented or halted, might lead to genocide;
2. Acting as a mechanism of early warning to the Secretary-General, and through him to the Security Council, by bringing to their attention situations that could potentially result in genocide;
3. Making recommendations to the Security Council, through the Secretary-General, on actions to prevent or halt genocide; and
4. Liaising with the United Nations system on activities for the prevention of genocide and work to enhance the United Nations' capacity to analyze and manage information regarding genocide or related crimes."[137]

The Office's Analysis Framework developed to determine the risk of genocide in given situations and encourages others to adopt this framework and analyze genocide risk. The eight

---

[137]Office of the Special Adviser on the Prevention of Genocide.

factors, cumulatively increase the risk of genocide over time. The triggering factors, included in

the list are signals or indicators:

"1. Tense inter-group relations, including a record of discrimination and/or other human rights violations committed against a group;
2. Weak institutional capacity to prevent genocide, such as the lack of an independent judiciary, ineffective national human rights institutions, the absence of international actors capable of protecting vulnerable groups, a lack of impartial security forces and media;
3. The presence of illegal arms and armed elements;
4. Underlying political, economic, military or other motivation to target a group;
5. Circumstances that facilitate perpetration of genocide, such as a sudden or gradual strengthening of the military or security apparatus;
6. Acts that could be elements of genocide, such as such as killings, abduction and disappearances, torture, rape and sexual violence, 'ethnic cleansing' or pogroms or the deliberate deprivation of food; evidence of the 'intent to destroy in whole or in part';
7. Triggering factors, such as elections."[138]

**Sentinel Satellite Project**

The Sentinel Satellite Project's (SSP) methodology uses, "commercial satellite imagery,

academic analysis, and advocacy to promote human rights in Sudan and South Sudan and serve as

an early warning system for impending crisis."[139] The Satellite Sentinel Project synthesizes

evidence from satellite imagery, data pattern analysis, and ground sourcing to produce reports.

Specifically the SSP monitors six areas of crisis and documenting:

1. Bombardment and Attacks
2. Early Warning of Attacks on Civilians
3. Evidence of Apparent Mass Graves
4. Evidence of Forced Displacement
5. Tracking Compliance in the Sudans
6. Village Razings
To illustrate SSP's method, bombardment and attacks are used as an example. First,

imagery was used to capture evidence of Sudanese Armed Forces (SAF) military aircraft

midflight, and alleged battle damage of their effects by looking at smoke plumes and signs of

---

[138]Office of the Special Adviser on the Prevention of Genocide.

[139]Satellite Sentinel Project, "Our Story."

damage caused by artillery, aircraft, and transport vehicles from the SAF. Second, journalists reports and documents reported upon the incidents. Next, those reports and analysis of imagery exposed the types of weapons and arms capabilities of SAF, and together validate claims of SAF caused damage and violations of human rights. The way in which SSP knows how attacks occur is by comparing before and after imagery and marrying it up with on the ground reports and battle damage assessments. Analysts use crater and military effects analysis as evidence to how attacks occurred. These reports are useful for those who want to alert civilians before violent action occurs against civilians, or use this data as evidence for tendencies of future actions of the SAF.[140]

### Operational Satellite Application Programme (UNOSAT)

United Nations Institute for Training and Research (UNITAR) Operational Satellite Application Programme (UNOSAT) methodology first conducts preliminary research prior to conflict mapping and tracking. Next, UNOSAT obtains baseline information pertaining to geographic security issues, and then identifies areas of interest to acquire satellite imagery data, followed by analysis. Analysis consists mainly of "a variety of computational tools which combine both manual and automated change detection and feature extraction techniques."[141] Preliminary reports are the goal (one or two days); however, in certain situations, especially for investigations, reports can take longer (several months). Analytical findings are represented in several formats "written text, tables and graphs, detailed maps, and graphics illustrating spatial patterns." [142]

---

[140]Satellite Sentinel Project, "Our Story."

[141]United Nations Institute for Training and Research, *UNOSAT Brief: Satellite Applications for Human Security,* 9.

[142]Ibid.

UNOSAT analysis focuses on human security. The scope of the imagery analysis looks at "damaged or destroyed buildings (including hospitals, schools, residential neighborhoods and cultural and religious sites), as well as populations under threat, or militia deployments."[143] Human security analysis maintains two approaches: traditional post-conflict event analysis and dynamic conflict event monitoring.

Post-conflict event analysis compares a number of satellite images from pre-event images to post-event images for a change in detection processes that finalizes a post-conflict assessment upon the event. New satellite imagery requests, called "taskings", view locations of interest in some circumstances, while in other situations the working order uses archival materials collected earlier.[144] Reducing the complexity of aggregated security events poses one limitation for the use of this technique. Another limitation in observation occurs when major events during a time become part of the whole. Commercial VHR technology enables organizations to request the imagery for the time segments in question, instead of tasking satellite time.[145]

The other method, dynamic conflict event monitoring, engages with the improvements to commercial capabilities allowing for continuous conflict monitoring from VIIR satellites and processing computer power. Satellite monitoring has identified the following: unreported security incidents; rapid conflict zone changes; confirmation of unverified witness accounts; and insight into active and evolving conflict affecting civilian security.[146]

---

[143]Ibid.

[144]Ibid., 10.

[145]"Very high-resolution (VHR) satellite imagery is generally defined as imagery recorded at a spatial resolution of one metre or less. Image resolution refers to the size of the smallest detail on the surface of the Earth detected by the satellite. Thus, a satellite with a resolution of one meter can discern objects one metre across or greater. VHR is considered by UNOSAT to be the most suitable for human rights and human security applications, though lower resolution imagery can sometimes be used as well."

[146]United Nations Institute for Training and Research. *UNOSAT Brief,* 10.

Currently, the examples for monitoring are few; however, two categories exist to describe dynamic monitoring: civilian direct monitoring and direct security incident monitoring.[147] Active direct civilian monitoring follows risks to populations using satellite imagery at several collection points during short intervals. The analyzed data provides humanitarian and protective agencies reliable estimates of the situation based upon the following civilian threats: exposure to indirect fire; tracking rapid and mass scale civilian movement in conflict zones; relations of the ground fighting to civilian reactions and movements. UNOSAT acknowledges an example of this type of occurrence and monitoring of displaced persons in Sri Lanka in 2009. [148]

The other category, direct security incident monitoring, uses a conflict lifecycle as the approach. The intent of the approach is to expand the post-conflict scale and duration being monitored. Satellite monitoring provides more insight on specific sequencing of events, spots alleged cease-fire violations, and assists with legal ramifications to human rights obligations.[149]

UNOSAT's future research technologies use geospatial mapping for human security. They include new radar satellite sensors for VHR coverage using change techniques to cover gaps in satellite VHR coverage, and computational modeling for active fire locations; significant for finding early stages of conflict.

**WITNESS**

WITNESS's methodology uses videos and storytelling to expose the world to human rights abuses.[150] WITNESS uses bystander captured evidence from human rights activists around the world, and now uses a comprehensive training approach focusing on video advocacy. Their

---

[147]Ibid.

[148]Ibid.

[149]Ibid.

[150]WITNESS, "About Us: Our Mission."

program called, "Cameras everywhere" gives bystanders throughout the world the means for

reporting human rights abuses. Moreover, WITNESS puts their unique video advocacy resources

online, so they are adoptable and accessible to citizens around the world.[151] WITNESS's

"Cameras Everywhere" program sought a method to ensure human rights videographers were

effective, safe in practice, and following an ethical code to document human rights abuses:

> WITNESS' core methodology is called video advocacy, an approach we pioneered to use video as an integrated tool in human rights campaigns. Our experience with our partners has proven that powerful images and stories have an unrivaled, candid authority that can help promote awareness and prompt action when seen by the right people at the right time and place.[152]

**Amnesty International**

Amnesty International uses three tactics in their methodology: research; action; and

advocacy. Their use of independent reports uses rigorous research. They claim that they are

undisturbed by corporate and government influence which adds to their credibility. In action,

Amnesty uses campaigns and long-term casework to influence human rights concerns using

stories of at-risk individuals and reports this to the international media. Amnesty uses a program

called Science for Human Rights. This program uses technological advances in science to

advocate human rights campaigns. They use geospatial technology, such as satellite imagery, to

monitor human rights violations and conflict prevention. These allow access to inaccessible

conflict zones, show visual evidence, and present information in new ways.[153]

One program called Mapping Repression in Syria uses a website documenting field

investigations in Aleppo, Syria and shows the violations on a visual map. This map documents

government security forces and government backed forces such as Shabiha militia's violence and

---

[151]Ibid.

[152]WITNESS, *Video for Change Toolkit.*

[153]Amnesty International, "Science for Human Rights."

fire against civilian demonstrators. The map allows the user to view the incidents, pictures, and first hand reports on the internet.[154] After accumulating research, reports such as "All Out Repression" uses a link on the webpage, which essentially publishes the incidents and makes them available for .pdf download in several languages.[155] Another similar program Amnesty uses is called "Eyes on Darfur" which records the evidence in real-time of the destruction occurring within Darfur.[156]

**FEWER**

The Forum of Early Warning and Early Response-Africa (FEWER) uses an early warning and response system. Four elements of the system help to uncover warning signs: systematic training and capacity building; conflict monitoring, analysis, and reporting; policy response and strategy development; and raising awareness.

Training and Capacity Building relies upon accurate and reliable analysis through training others in the process. The two-step approach focuses first on the partner organizations, to ensure the mechanisms and institutional structures needs are available for the program, and engage with community institutions represented in the analysis--donors and policy makers. The second step of the approach trains on the FEWER Africa conflict analysis methodology.[157]

FEWER's Institutional Capacity Building uses local experience as the implementers and are those working with civil society and the community in West and Central Africa. Success

---

[154]Amnesty International, "News: Syria: From all-out repression to armed conflict in Aleppo," http://www.amnesty.org/en/news/syria-all-out-repression-armed-conflict-aleppo-2012-08-01 (accessed 15 August 2012).

[155]Amnesty International, "Syria: All-Out Repression: Purging Dissent in Aleppo, Syria," http://www.amnesty.org/en/library/info/MDE24/061/2012/en (accessed 15 August 2012).

[156]Amnesty International, "Eyes on Darfur." http://www.amnestyusa.org/research/science-for-human-rights/eyes-on-darfur (accessed 15 August 2012).

[157]FEWER. "Early Warning Early Response."

happens in the program when the institution supports the responsible parties for analysis. Also, success occurs when sustainable program outcomes occur where mechanisms and structures exist at those local levels. Legitimacy derives from delivering credible programs to the individuals it supports and for the donors it represents.[158]

FEWER's conflict analysis training deals with understanding conflict and peace generating factors for early warning analysis. FEWER assumed that a factual approach to early warning is flawed because different indicators have a number of differing ways that people in affected areas interpret them. Perception is as important as the facts and the analytical assumptions are the following:

> (a) conflict trends - (b) peace trends +/- (c) stakeholder trends = overall trends. On this basis, responses to conflict and peace developments, as well as stakeholder actions are defined. Therefore capacity building focuses on understanding root causes, proximate causes, and triggers of conflict, peace indicators, and stakeholder analysis of interests, agendas, and capacities.[159]

FEWER's Conflict Monitoring Analysis and Reporting provides evidence to inform responses to conflict and gives civil society groups opportunity to influence decision-making. This process seeks to predict future scenarios and give time for preventive action. The on-going monitoring and conflict analysis produces three types of reports: annual baseline of the situations with risk assessments; regular early warning reports; and policy briefs. Additionally, the produced artifacts incorporate "methodological input from the project partners and other FEWER Africa members."[160]

Finally, FEWER's methodology contains Policy Response and Strategic Development. Local conflict and peace analyses work to create responsive strategies where effective preventive

---

[158]Ibid.

[159]Ibid.

[160]Ibid.

action requires an integrated approach. Dialogue between civil society groups, state, and non-state actors addresses responses to conflict.

> An effective methodology for planning and implementing integrated responses to local conflict situations requires: (a) on-going political monitoring and surveying of peace-building activities (b) multi-actor strategic planning exercises; and (c) on-going policy outreach and policy briefing meetings with policy-makers and other stakeholders.[161]

**FIDH**

Federation international des ligue des droits de l'homme (FIDH) International Federation for Human Rights, uses the Universal Declaration of Human Rights (UDHR) as the profile for warning signs and indictors that are viewed, analyzed, and reported. Warning signs and indicators are therefore, violations of the articles of the Universal Declaration of Human Rights.

FIDH's mission to protect and support human rights defenders accomplishes its goals through a joint program called the Observatory for the Protection of Human Rights Defenders with the World Organization Against Torture (OMCT), a program started in 1997. The program supports defenders and their abilities to act. Modes of action include:

> Emergency alerts (urgent appeals, press releases, open or closed letters to the authorities), documentation of violations and an analysis of the causes (international fact-finding missions), direct support (material assistance, relocation, trial observation, defense missions, solidarity missions) and the mobilisation of inter-governmental organisations and public opinion (communications, direct advocacy, campaigns, publication of an annual report).[162]

Daily alerts (urgent appeals, press releases, letter to authorities) about the harassment of defenders enables mobilization of State and international actors and media about the situation and cases of harassment. The recommendations amounted to putting together fact-finding missions and advocacy to protect human rights defenders in the public, and fight against government stigmatization and measures to delegitimize them as political enemies. During armed conflicts

---

[161]Ibid.

[162]FIDH, 12.

and political crises, FIDH ensured the safety of defenders so that close monitoring could take place. Assassinations of defenders in Africa called for actions and FIDH attempted to protect defenders against monitoring while simultaneously pointing out human rights violations.[163]

Conflict zone documentation of human rights situations remains complicated as authorities often refuse FIDH on their territory. This is the case with Sudan and Somalia. In Darfur, FIDH constantly updates the international community to ensure protection of civilians and prevent impunity for perpetrators. Documentation therefore, works as both methods for sanctions and prevention.

In the Democratic Republic of Congo (DRC), the conflict problems were being well documented by other international organizations. Therefore, FIDH shifted their efforts to fight for policy against impunity for perpetrators of serious crimes, and expanded their support in the region by streamlining their efforts and providing another service, instead of a redundant mechanism.

FIDH chose to monitor fragile security situations for countries in transition and post-conflict because the risk to conflict and risk of human rights protection required close monitoring. They selected Niger, Guinea, and Burundi for this. Their aim was to mobilize the African Union and the African Courts on Human and Peoples' Rights.[164]

In efforts to strengthen members and partners FIDH supports human rights defenders. They do this because there is an inherent problem and risk to reporting human rights violations for reporters on-site. The field workers collect vital information but are unable to store or communicate easily or securely. FIDH offered a set of tools to allow reporting to occur despite the obvious setbacks. This was accomplished with secure messaging platforms with several

---

[163]Ibid., 12-14.

[164]Ibid., 46-48.

66

language interfaces. FIDH also helps defenders with Internet circumventing censorship solutions that avoids States who restrict access to those who try to report on abuses.

During the revolutions in the Arab world in 2011, FIDH enable their partners by creating websites for ATFD, a Tunisian organization, to allow them access to bloggers who could locally monitor the situation. Also, FIDH supported the Damascus Center for Human Rights Studies so that it was better structured to relay information regarding human rights situations from national/international NGOs within Syria.[165]

FIDH reported a need to build capacity to mobilize the public and develop the protective impact and influence of FIDH. One of the objectives was to strengthen communications with mass media through press releases or direct contact with journalists on specific topics. The objective was to put FIDH in a role as a news agency specialized in human rights. To validate FIDH's success as subject matter experts in this area, they were approached by 300 journalists with requests for information and interviews specific to these areas of interest. This role allows FIDH to remain visible and to "make the news", and gives them the ability to alert to early warning.[166]

### Human Right Watch (HRW)

Human Rights Watch (HRW) methodology investigates 90 countries for human rights abuses. They actively research, report, and advocate change. They choose their focus countries and the issues to address. HRW bases this upon their intuition and experience, and where they believe they can make a positive change. They respond to emergencies; however, they challenge standing or steadily deteriorating human rights problems worldwide.

---

[165]Ibid., 69-70.

[166]Ibid., 73-74.

HRW uses 80 staff researchers. "The researchers work to an established, proven, and consistent methodology based on information gathering from a broad range of sources, and with field-based research at its core."[167] Some researchers are permanent field workers, proximate to their research. They are on mission conducting field investigations, interviewing victims and witnesses. The purpose to these investigations is to put the human story as the reason for reporting and advocacy. Research cooperation works with civil society activists, lawyers, and journalists. HRW also seeks access to government officials. Developments are followed/monitored using mass media research, peer organization output, research community findings, and contacts in the local activists' field (via phone/email).[168]

HRW researches the problem, and then decides on an advocacy approach specific to the problem. In addition, the process identifies who is responsible for stopping human rights violations, who should provide redress, the steps both need to take, and whom else may provide influence and bear upon the situation.

HRW's researchers organize geographically and thematically. Five geographic divisions give global insight to the following countries: Africa, Americas, Asia, Europe & Central Asia, and Middle East & North Africa, and U.S. (special program). Themes provide depth and focus and include the following: Arms; Business & Human Rights; Children's Rights; Terrorism & Counterterrorism; Health & Human Rights; International Justice; Lesbian, Gay, Bisexual &Transgender Rights; Refugees; and Women's Rights.

Institutionalized reporting and management accuracy comes in the form of controlled supervision. Divisional program directors and core departments manage high organizational

---

[167]Human Rights Watch, "Methodology."
[168]Ibid.

standards for accuracy, balance, and persuasiveness. Two examples of managerial departments functioning in this capacity are the Legal & Policy Office and the Program Office.[169]

HRW's research strategies or topics of research exploration are premised on the guiding principles found within the organization. Initial stages differ in response to an emergency human rights violation versus a long-standing one. In emergencies, documentation of the violations/abuses requires geographically located researchers, using regional specialists (in the country or the theme), or using dedicated emergency researchers. Conversely, for long-term issues, researchers explore through deployment, their capability to research the country or issue with detailed background research. The aim familiarizes the researcher with the context and subtleties of the subjects prior to interviewing victims and witnesses.[170]

Goals for initial stage research are the following and are relative to an incident or human rights violation: developing a thorough holistic understanding of the incident or human rights violation; and to gain a strong sense of the local political, social, and cultural context. Moreover, researchers frame violations with respect to international human rights violations and humanitarian law. Contextualizing the situation and violations assists in the following: identification of possible victims and witnesses for testimony, reaching out to all actors in the violation, and identifying advocacy targets. Primarily, familiarization with understanding the situation and local conditions involves accessing and communicating with relevant local network contacts and actors.

HRW researchers rely most heavily on relevant contacts from the initial stages of incidents and throughout the research to identify victims and witnesses for testimony. Thus they

---

[169]Ibid.
[170]Ibid.

gain a relevant research population. The lists of important contacts are the following: allies in human rights activists and civil society members; "lawyers, journalists, doctors, student groups, government officials, diplomats, representatives of international nongovernmental organizations and international experts, to exchange/solicit information and to help identify witnesses, victims, recommendations, and advocacy targets."[171]

Other background research information provides context and comes from study of international humanitarian law and human rights laws; domestic and local laws; U.N. and international organization data; academic and policy studies; NGO reporting and reports; and mass media reporting.

HRW has a method for identifying research locations. The goal for the HRW approach is to create an accurate picture of the incident or repeated human rights incident by following what occurred by obtaining the right amount of information that informs upon the situation.

Fact-finding includes interviewing victims and attempting to gain other sides of the story. Researchers go on location for data pertaining to alleged but plausible violations known to have occurred or ongoing violations. Limitations may exist with the security conditions and time, which affect the overall research. Before research investigation and missions, HRW evaluates the security risk to develop communications and security plans. In situations of major armed conflict and violence, the researchers remain as long as their security allows.[172]

Systematic and repeated human rights violations indicate and identify the problem areas that need further research. HRW conducts background research to assist in understanding the problems. Background research consists of extensive literature reviews, mass media reporting,

---

[171]Ibid.

[172]Ibid.

interviews with experts on the specific topic, local human rights partners/organizations, academics, and civil society. Local actors assist with access to witnesses and victims for interviews. Sometimes this may occur in groupings, for example, refugee camps and hospitals.[173]

Existing studies assist in the triangulation of where to conduct valid research. In some cases, demographics assist to get a broad list of where to conduct interviews. Some examples of the data used in HRW's past are the following:

> Using HIV prevalence rates to determine which regions of Russia to visit to investigate access to evidence-based drug dependence treatment for injection drug users using school district discipline rates along with demographic statistics to select districts in Texas to visit to research corporal punishment in high schools.[174]

HRW uses interviewing standards. HRW researcher interviews occur when investigating human rights abuses to understand what occurred. HRW seeks direct interviews with witnesses and victims. The interviews give the witnesses and victims a broader audience. The interviews help HRW develop recommendations to authorities for cessation and redress of human rights violations.

Research interviews begin with direct actors with knowledge of the incident or those with relevant information about the rights violation (subject matter experts) in order to understand the social, political, and cultural contexts reported. Local human rights organizations, activists, local NGOs/International organizations, and members of civil society assist in the initial discussions to locate actors to interview. Corroborating information with interview accounts occurs with the following individuals: "UN representatives, journalists, doctors and medical experts, lawyers and legal experts, community leaders, law enforcement officials, diplomats, and civil society leaders

---

[173]Ibid.

[174]Ibid.

in order to corroborate information from witnesses and victims."[175] HRW in an attempt to get all perspectives also seeks out government officials, military leaders, rebels, militia groups, and any accused perpetrators for furthering explanations of incidents, and to communicate HRW's concerns about the reported situations. The attempt is made, even though historically access has not been granted, or requests for information have been unanswered. Lastly, in some cases, interviews were too risky to conduct because of the negative security risks to researchers.[176]

Because each human right violation is unique, no uniform interview technique or methodology is used by HRW. The principles; however, are standard: the need to find the truth, to corroborate statement veracity, protect security and dignity of witnesses, and remain impartial.[177]

The most commonly used techniques for interviewing witnesses and victims are the following: interviews in private settings, face-to-face with researcher, focusing interview details on what occurred. The purpose of private settings protects witness confidentiality, and helps interviewees give truthful statements in an independent environment. Researchers ask other witnesses the same questions about the same incidents to corroborate facts, confirm similar accounts, and expose falsifications or exaggerations.[178]

A common interview technique confirming veracity, questions in order to gain insight into the details of incidents. The details assist with determining if the information was from a witnessed event or from hearsay. Questions ask details about names, ages, locations, and times. In cases where a previous interview was taken, clarification about earlier statements are asked.

_____

[175]Ibid.

[176]Ibid.

[177]Ibid.

[178]Ibid.

Other witnesses are asked the same questions about the same incidents to check veracity. The logic is that many interviews present the same details if true, if not, then false.[179]

HRW's interview standards help to protect their interviewees. Researchers avoid further trauma to those suffering abuse, and ensure their researchers are trained in communication sensitivity. Also, researchers establish secure and private settings, inform interviewees to the purpose and scope of interview, and obtain consent. The options to opt out or quit the interview at anytime is also briefed to those interviewed as well as a standard to ensure anonymity and confidentiality. Rescheduling, cancellation, or termination of interviews may be determined by the researcher if the emotional state of the interviewee not emotionally ready.

The interviews are conducted in the primary language of the interviewee. Often HRW representatives are fluent in the language. Consultants with fluency in local language and dialect are used in cases where this is not present in HRW, usually with interpreters with former associations and working in the same field of advocacy. Questions and answers are translated verbatim allowing clarity in follow-up questions. [180]

When possible, interviews occur in person. When unavailable in this venue, then other methods occur, such as telephone or other means. The interview setting reflects in the final reporting annotations.

HRW has non-interview standards. Apart from interviews, HRW reviews mass media reporting, domestic legislation, international law, policy papers, academic and civil society reports. These occur in the initial stages and continue throughout research. To make cases, HRW uses trial materials, government reports, and convictions and sentencing. HRW combines these

---

[179]Ibid.
[180]Ibid.

with other data collection from the UN, regional intergovernmental agencies, and domestic government to prove human rights abuses exist and to what extent. An example follows:

> Using US criminal sentencing data to prove racial discrepancies in the sentencing of juveniles to life without parole or using patient payment records from hospitals in Burundi to prove inequitable and unethical treatment of patients. There have also been instances where Human Watch Researchers have collected and analyzed primary data, such as in a report enumerating war crimes in Kosovo that contains our own analysis of trends in the data.[181]

While in the field, researchers obtain information and data not part of interviewing, but examining the locations of incidents using forensic type methods. Photographs of injured bodies, on-location destruction, spent ammunition casings, and crater and explosion analysis have assisted. Also, HRW uses GPS coordinates and satellite imagery in analysis and exposes abuses. HRW researchers are trained to use other methods besides interviews to document.[182]

HRW noted their methodology challenges. The first speaks to closed-society research. Closed society research tried to access countries, such as Iran or North Korea, who close their borders completely to HRW's researchers. The challenges and security risk to both researchers and interviewees make this a difficult task. Data collection challenges include: identifying rights violations, understanding local context, finding witnesses and victims, and finding feasible recommendations and advocacy opportunities.[183]

Closed region information gathering uses different techniques. Interviews are often conducted on telephone or on-line communications. HRW pays particular attention to verifying the identities of victims and witnesses using the same corroborative techniques explained above.

---

[181]Ibid.

[182]Ibid.

[183]Ibid.

Another method uses interviews from witnesses just arriving from closed areas. Traditionally this has been a good method for information about closed regions. For example, HRW interviews at refugee camps, displaced person locations, and military and rebel outposts.

Close region satellite monitoring assists HRW to expose human rights abuses. It shows before and after effects of violence and conflict, destruction of villages, and mass movements of people. Reports to HRW have been verified with imagery to confirm incidents in closed regions. Time stamped images give before and after imagery that can prove attacks occurred.

> Ethnic cleansing" and genocide in Rwanda and the Balkans prompted the need for both real-time reporting of atrocities and in-depth documentation of cases to press for international prosecutions, which became possible for the first time in the 1990s. Human Rights Watch has supported and critiqued the international tribunals for the former Yugoslavia and Rwanda, sought prosecutions of abusive leaders including Augusto Pinochet of Chile and Hissene Habre of Chad, and played a prominent role in the drafting of the Rome Statute to create the International Criminal Court.[184]

HRW pressures terrorist organizations and their supporters. At the same time, HRW monitors counterterrorism laws, policies, and practices to observe if violations of human rights occur. [185]

Finally, HRW uses traditional fact finding with researchers on the ground with new technologies to bridge the gap in documenting and reporting human rights violations worldwide. They apply their research methodology in other areas such as economic, social, cultural, education, and housing rights.[186]

**International Crisis Group (ICG)**

---

[184]Ibid.

[185]Ibid.

[186]Ibid.

ICG reports on conflict prevention and resolution across the world for issues dealing with Islamist terrorism, nuclear proliferation, local conflict issues, and problems dealing with failed, failing, and fragile states. They have six main roles:

1. Early warning alerts through *CrisisWatch*'s bulletin and specific crisis alerts within the bulletin.

2. Behind the scenes contribution for advice to peace negotiations, with past performance in Sudan, Burundi, Northern Uganda, Zimbabwe

3. Detailed analysis and advice on policy issues dealing with potential global conflicts . Helping policy makers, UN Security Council, regional organizations, donors, influencers, and at-risk countries to better prevent, manage, and resolve conflict. Also, assisting with rebuilding efforts after conflict.

4. Information on developments on conflict, mass violence and terrorism to policy makers. Examples include Jemash Islamiyah in Indonesia and jihadi groups in Pakistan and Afghanistan.

5. Offer strategic thinking about the world's intractable conflicts to challenge the prevailing ideas. Examples included: Iran nuclear issues, Islamism worldwide, and Arab-Israeli conflict.

6. Supporting rules-based vice force-based international order. Influencing UN resolutions and international institutional structures, especially in relation to the norm of the Responsibility to Protect.[187]

Through 130 staff members on five different continents, Crisis Group uses field-based analysis for high level advocacy to prevent and resolve deadly conflict. They base their approach

---

[187]International Crisis Group, "About Crisis Group."

on field workers located within the countries at risk of outbreak, escalation, or a return to violent conflict. Information and assessments come from the field. They make recommendations to key international decision-makers.

Additionally, Crisis Group publishes the situations of most significant conflict potential through a distributed system of email and their website. The Crisis Group Board with former European Commissioner for External Relations and a former U.S. Ambassador bring credibility to the reports as they take them to senior policy-makers. The president of Crisis Group is the former U.N. High Commissioner for Human Rights and Chief Prosecutor for the International Criminal Tribunals for the former Yugoslavia and Rwanda.[188]

### Genocide Watch

Genocide Watch uses a methodology from Dr. Stanton's "Eight Stages of Genocide." Genocide Watch acts as the coordinating agent organization for The International Alliance to End Genocide (IAEG), which is an international coalition of organizations. IAEG educates the public and policy makers about the causes, processes, and warning signs of genocide. They do this to create institutional and political will to prevent and stop genocide and to prosecute perpetrators of genocide.

Genocide Watch has objectives in education, prediction, prevention, intervention, and justice. Education plays the role to raise awareness to specific high-risk situations and genocide as a global issue. Prediction uses models such as Dr. Stanton's "Eight Stages of Genocide" as an instrument to analyze situations for educational, policy analysis, and advocacy purposes. Genocide Watch monitors high-risk areas where genocide is alleged and declare Genocide

---

[188]International Crisis Group, *Tajinkistan: The Changing Insurgent Threats.*

Watches, Warnings, and Emergencies. With these declarations come recommendations for options for governments, international organizations, and NGOs to prevent genocide.

Genocide Watch's option papers for policy makers recommend specific prevention measures and actions to prevent genocide in high-risk areas using their understanding of the genocide process. They use resources from IAEG, other international organizations and collaborate with field workers.

Intervention becomes necessary when mass atrocity occurs and actions are required to stop genocide. Genocide Watch works through the IAEG promoting quick response by the U.N., regional, and authorized national forces. Intervention through the means of mandates and funding assist in their process to gain the political will for intervention.

Genocide Watch supports national justice systems, special national/international tribunals, International Criminal Court, and truth and reconciliation commissions. The purpose of these programs aim to get justice for victims and survivors, while punishing perpetrators, deterring genocides, and assisting in the transition of divided societies into peace.[189]

## The Indicators or Warning Signs

It is important for the research to discover that international organizations monitor relevant early warning signs and indicators. Observing the literature review, the case studies, and their experience have shown that indeed they are looking at the right signs. Analysis of the international organizations viewed, displayed common warning signs that derive mainly from the United Nations, Special Advisor on the Prevention of Genocide (See Appendix D, OSAPG Analysis). The first seven factors of the analysis framework deal mainly with historical risk data

---

[189]Genocide Watch, "About Us."

and information--mainly what current genocidal risk situation resides within a State. Whereas, the eighth uses upcoming scenarios and predicts problems in future risk events related to genocide and mass atrocity. Each of the international organizations seemed informed by the Analysis Framework.

The Sentinel Satellite Project looked at possible threats to civilians and evidence of pending mass violence from satellite imagery and focused on evidence such as, "warning signs-- elevated roads for moving heavy armor, lengthened airstrips for landing attack aircraft, build-ups of troops, tanks, and artillery preparing for invasion."[190] UNOSAT with a similar mission conducts preliminary reporting of conflict zones or areas of interest and damaged and/or destroyed buildings to including hospitals, schools, residential neighborhoods, and cultural and religious sites. [191] They also considered populations under threat and militia deployments.[192] "UNOSAT addresses three main homogeneous user systems: Humanitarian Affairs and Relief Coordination (Crisis & Situational Mapping, Damage and Impact Assessment, Human Security); Monitoring (Safety and Security, Human Rights, Territorial Planning and Monitoring); [and] Capacity Development & Technical Assistance (In-country Project Development & Implementation)."[193]

Another way to view warning signs constitutes searching for human rights abuses and reporting through captured video. "WITNESS empowers human rights defenders to use video to fight injustice, and to transform personal stories of abuse into powerful tools that can pressure

---

[190]Satellite Sentinel Project. "Documenting the Crisis."

[191]United Nations Institute for Training and Research. UNOSAT Brief, 9.

[192]Ibid.

[193]United Nations Institute for Training and Research, *What We Do.*

those in power or with power to act."[194] Human Rights Watch also looks for human rights abuses by interviewing within refugee camps, military and rebel outposts; the use of satellite imagery, and investigating property destruction. They bridge a gap between media, human rights, and technology by using innovation to the traditional approaches to advocacy. [195]

FIDH and Amnesty International use the Universal Declaration of Human Rights as the model for observing and reporting early warning signs. FIDH also uses fact finding missions to viewing the violations if the UDHR, observes countries in transition that might resume conflict, and countries facing new elections after conflict.[196] FEWER, similar to FIDH, views conflict and peace generating factors, and root causes, proximate causes, and triggers of conflict, peace indicators, and stakeholder analysis of interests, agendas, and capacities. [197]

International Crisis Group (ICG) reports on conflict prevention and resolution across the world for issues dealing with Islamist terrorism, nuclear proliferation, local conflict issues, and problems dealing with failed, failing, and fragile states.[198] ICG views conflict as it pertains to the deterioration of Peace and Justice, Gender, Climate Change, and the Responsibility to Protect.[199]

Lastly, Genocide Watch uses the Dr. Stanton's "8 Stages of Genocide" as a prediction instrument to code analysis of at-risk countries and signal warnings and indicators of genocide.[200]

---

[194]WITNESS, "About Us: Our Mission."

[195]Ibid.

[196]FIDH, 4.

[197]FEWER, "Early Warning Early Response."

[198]International Crisis Group, "About Crisis Group."

[199]International Crisis Group,."Key Issues." August 20, 2012.

[200]Genocide Watch, "About Us."

# The Purpose of Warning Signs and Indicators

It is important to understand if the warning signs and indicators observed, in fact, predict mass atrocity and genocide. If they do not, then their purpose did not fulfill the mission of observation. The common purpose of early warning signs and indicators, for international organizations, were of prevention. Another common view was for documentation of the early warning signs and indicators. Several other purposes that tie into prevention team up to bring the issues to policy action. This is where third parties meet with policy/decision-makers and where each can portray facts and better illuminate the problems and issues surrounding R2P and genocide prevention. The three main areas for the United Nations, Special Adviser on the Prevention of Genocide were **raising awareness, alerting, and advocacy**. All of the international organizations used this model. In addition, the UN sought to eliminate political/economic inequalities to promote a sense of belonging,[201] and for decision-making that involved collective action, making judgments on whether peaceful means remain inadequate, if national authorities are failing to protect, and whether to bring up the issues with the Security Council or the General Assembly.[202] Without verified facts, these are needless goals that do not meet R2P requirements nor assist in genocide prevention.

The Satellite Sentinel Project's purpose was to alert the public, press, policymakers, major news organizations, and social media; especially, Twitter and Facebook. The stated purpose is to observe alleged atrocity as it develops and unfolds and to "document, deter, and seek accountability for war criminals and mass atrocities."[203] Similarly, UNOSAT's goal is to make satellite solutions and geographic information easily accessible to the UN family and to

---

[201]Office of the UN Special Adviser on the Prevention of Gencode, "Overview of OSAPG."

[202]United Nations General Assembly, 2.

[203]Satellite Sentinel Project, "Documenting the Crisis."

experts worldwide who work at reducing the impact of crises and disasters and help nations plan for sustainable development."[204] UNOSAT believed that geographic analysis positively affects "processes, initiatives and organizations with a mission to protect human rights and uphold international humanitarian law, thus improving overall human security internationally."[205] The contribution of the system has human security application in these five areas:

- Advocacy

- Mitigation and Prevention

- Enhancing Field Investigations

- Remote Fact Finding

- Peace and Reconciliation[206]

WITNESS video images have a purpose to support activism, as a tool for change, [207], empower and expose injustice, empower activists to protect and defend human rights[208], document human rights violations[209], ensure transparency, good governance, and accountability are upheld within society.[210] WITNESS sees their unique contribution as a world authority for best practices in the use of video monitoring, reporting, training, and the expertise on human rights abuses.[211]

---

[204]United Nations Institute for Training and Research, *Who We Are.*

[205]United Nations Institute for Training and Research. *UNOSAT Brief,* 5.

[206]Ibid.

[207]WITNESS, *Cameras Everywhere: Current challenges and opportunities at the intersection of human rights, video and technology,* 8.

[208]Ibid.

[209]Ibid., 10.

[210]Ibid.

[211]WITNESS, "About Us: Our Mission."

Amnesty International has several purposes. They aimed to unite people to fight for human rights using three tactics: research; action; and advocacy. Amnesty publishes independent reports based upon rigorous research, undisturbed by corporate and government influence and uses campaigns and long-term casework to influence human rights concerns using stories of at-risk individuals to the international media. Another purpose is to hold the attention of government officials, policy makers, corporations, and international institutions. Finally, as advocates, Amnesty promotes legislation and policies to advance human rights by integrating media and grassroots mobilization that assists to protect individuals and free prisoners of conscience.[212]

Similarly, Human Right Watch's purpose uses advocacy and supports human rights international laws. HRW defends and protects human rights, supports the oppressed and holds perpetrators accountable for crimes, produces rigorous and objective investigations, builds strategic and targeted advocacy with intense pressure for action, and try to change legal and moral structures for better justice and security for everyone in the world .[213] Additionally, HRW uses early warning to prevent discrimination by supporting victims and activists, uphold political freedom, protect people from inhumane wartime conduct, and to bring justice to perpetrators. [214] Moreover, HRW's purpose also investigates and exposes human rights violations; holding abusers accountable, challenge governments and power brokers to end abusive practices and respect international human rights law, and enlists the support of the public and international community for human rights for everyone.[215]

_____

[212]Ibid.

[213]Human Rights Watch, "About Us."

[214]Ibid.

[215]Ibid.

Early warning supports FIDH's purpose to defend civil, political, economic and cultural rights, established from the Universal Declaration of Human Rights, acting in legal and political fields for implementation of international instruments to protect human rights and for human rights implementation. They are a federalist movement acting through national member and partner organizations while working with local civil societies to identify local obstacles and mobilize support to overcome them.[216]

FEWER's purpose is to provide conflict analysis for use by policy makers, [217] and "ensure that local, regional and international actors participate in and 'own' conflict prevention and peacebuilding activities."[218] Early warning and response systems base upon these elements and purposes: systematic training and capacity building; conflict monitoring, analysis, and reporting; policy response and strategy development; and to raise awareness. [219]

The purposes for International Crisis Group create production of analytical reports with recommendations for key international decision makers, publication of Crisis Watch Bulletin, which provides regular updates on significant or potential conflicts in the world. Also, ICG uses early warning materials to generate support from governments and the media for policy prescription to conflict, and using their reports, the Crisis Group Board, makes recommendations to senior policy makers around the world. [220]

Lastly, Genocide Watch's objectives are in education, prediction, prevention, intervention, and justice. "Genocide Watch exists to predict, prevent, stop, and punish genocide

---

[216]FIDH, 4.

[217]FEWER, "FEWER Africa."

[218]Ibid.

[219]FEWER, "Early Warning Early Response."

[220]International Crisis Group, Asia Report No 204, 21.

and other forms of mass murder."[221] Genocide Watch raise awareness to potential and actual genocide to influence public policy and build an international movement to prevent and stop genocide.[222]

A tool was devised to demonstrate both the early warning signs/indicators and purpose of the international organizations researched to better illustrate the commonalities and differences. See Appendix F, Analysis of Third Party EW and Purpose.

----

[221]Genocide Watch, "About Us."
[222]Ibid.

# APPENDIX D

 ## OFFICE OF THE UN SPECIAL ADVISER ON THE PREVENTION OF GENOCIDE (OSAPG)

### ANALYSIS FRAMEWORK

**Legal definition of genocide**

Genocide is defined in Article 2 of the Convention on the Prevention and Punishment of the Crime of Genocide (1948) *as "any of the following acts committed with intent to destroy, in whole or in part, a national, ethnical, racial or religious group, as such: killing members of the group; causing serious bodily or mental harm to members of the group; deliberately inflicting on the group conditions of life calculated to bring about its physical destruction in whole or in part[1]; imposing measures intended to prevent births within the group; [and] forcibly transferring children of the group to another group."*

**Elements of the framework**

The Analysis Framework comprises eight categories of factors that the OSAPG uses to determine whether there may be a risk of genocide in a given situation. The eight categories of factors are not ranked, and the absence of information relating to one or more categories does not necessarily indicate the absence of a risk of genocide; what is significant is the cumulative effect of the factors. Where these factors are effectively addressed, no longer exist or are no longer relevant, the risk of genocide is assumed to decrease.

**Framework**

| Factors and explanation | |
| --- | --- |
| **1. Inter-group relations, including record of discrimination and/or other human rights violations committed against a group** | *Issues to be analyzed here include:* <br><br> • Relations between and among groups in terms of tensions, power and economic relations, including perceptions about the targeted group; <br> • Existing and past conflicts over land, power, security and expressions of group identity, such as language, religion and culture; <br> • Past and present patterns of discrimination against members of any group which could include: <br>    o Serious discriminatory practices, for instance, the compulsory identification of members of a particular group, imposition of taxes/fines, permission required for social activities such as marriage, compulsory birth-control, the systematic exclusion of groups from positions of power, employment in State institutions and/or key professions[2]; <br>    o Significant disparities in socio-economic indicators showing a pattern of deliberate exclusion from economic resources and social and political life. <br> • Overt justification for such discriminatory practices; <br> • History of genocide or related serious and massive human rights violations against a particular group; denial by the perpetrators; <br> • References to past human rights violations committed against a possible perpetrator group as a justification for genocidal acts against the targeted group in the future. |

---

[1] It might be necessary to determine if all or only a part of the group at risk within a specific geographical location is being targeted. The aim of the Genocide Convention is to prevent the intentional destruction of entire human groups, and the part targeted must be significant enough (substantial) to have an impact on the group as a whole. The substantiality requirement both captures genocide's defining character as a crime of massive proportions (numbers) and reflects the Convention's concern with the impact the destruction of the targeted part will have on the overall survival of the group (emblematic).
[2] This could include security, law enforcement or oversight apparatus, such as police, army and judiciary.

| 2. Circumstances that affect the capacity to prevent genocide | Structures that exist to protect the population and deter genocide include effective legislative protection; independent judiciary and effective national human rights institutions, presence of international actors such as UN operations capable of protecting vulnerable groups, neutral security forces and independent media. *Issues to be analyzed here include*: <br><br>• Existing structures; <br>• The effectiveness of those structures; <br>• Whether vulnerable groups have genuine access to the protection afforded by the structures; <br>• Patterns of impunity and lack of accountability for past crimes committed against the targeted groups; <br>• Other options for obtaining protection against genocide, e.g. presence of peacekeepers in a position to defend the group, or seeking asylum in other countries. |
|---|---|
| 3. Presence of illegal arms and armed elements | *The issues to be analyzed here include:* <br><br>• Whether there exists a capacity to perpetrate genocide - especially, but not exclusively, by killing; <br>• How armed groups are formed, who arms them and what links they have to state authorities, if any; <br>• In cases of armed rebellions or uprising, whether a state has justified targeting groups from which armed actors have drawn their membership. |
| 4. Motivation of leading actors in the State/region; acts which serve to encourage divisions between national, racial, ethnic, and religious groups | *The issues to be analyzed here include:* <br><br>• Underlying political, economic, military or other motivation to target a group and to separate it from the rest of the population; <br>• The use of exclusionary ideology and the construction of identities in terms of "us" and "them" to accentuate differences; <br>• Depiction of a targeted group as dangerous, disloyal, a security or economic threat or as unworthy or inferior so as to justify action against the group; <br>• Propaganda campaigns and fabrications about the targeted group used to justify acts against a targeted group by use of dominant, controlled media or "mirror politics"[3]; <br>• Any relevant role, whether active or passive, of actors outside the country (e.g., other Governments, armed groups based in neighboring countries, refugee groups or *diasporas*) and respective political or economic motivations. |
| 5. Circumstances that facilitate perpetration of genocide (dynamic factors) | *Issues to be analyzed here include:* <br><br>Any development of events, whether gradual or sudden, that suggest a trajectory towards the perpetration of genocidal violence, or the existence of a longer term plan or policy to commit genocide. Examples: <br><br>• Sudden or gradual strengthening of the military or security apparatus; creation of or increased support to militia groups (e.g., sudden increases in arms flow) in the absence of discernible legitimate threats; <br>• Attempts to reduce or eradicate diversity within the security apparatus; <br>• Preparation of local population to use them to perpetrate acts; <br>• Introduction of legislation derogating the rights of a targeted group; <br>• Imposition of emergency or extraordinary security laws and facilities that erode civil rights and liberties; |

---

[3] "Mirror politics" is a common strategy to create divisions by fabricating events whereby a person accuses others of what he or she does or wants to do.

| | |
|---|---|
| | • Sudden increase in inflammatory rhetoric or hate propaganda, especially by leaders, that sets a tone of impunity, even if it does not amount to incitement to genocidal violence in itself;<br>• Permissive environment created by ongoing armed conflict that could facilitate access to weapons and commission of genocide. |
| **6. Genocidal acts** | *Issues to be analyzed here include:*<br><br>• Acts that could be obvious "elements" of the crime of genocide as defined in Article 6 of the Rome Statute,[4] such as killings, abduction and disappearances, torture, rape and sexual violence; 'ethnic cleansing' or pogroms;[5]<br>• Less obvious methods of destruction, such as the deliberate deprivation of resources needed for the group's physical survival and which are available to the rest of the population, such as clean water, food and medical services;[6]<br>• Creation of circumstances that could lead to a slow death, such as lack of proper housing, clothing and hygiene or excessive work or physical exertion;<br>• Programs intended to prevent procreation, including involuntary sterilization, forced abortion, prohibition of marriage and long-term separation of men and women;<br>• Forcible transfer of children, imposed by direct force or through fear of violence, duress, detention, psychological oppression or other methods of coercion;<br>• Death threats or ill treatment that causes disfigurement or injury; forced or coerced use of drugs or other treatment that damages health. |
| **7. Evidence of intent "to destroy in whole or in part ..."[7]** | *Issues to be analyzed here include:*<br><br>• Statements amounting to hate speech [8] by those involved in a genocidal campaign;<br>• In a large-scale armed conflict, widespread and systematic nature of acts; intensity and scale of acts and invariability of killing methods used against the same protected group; types of weapons employed (in particular weapons prohibited under international law) and the extent of bodily injury caused;<br>• In a non-conflict situation, widespread and/or systematic discriminatory and targeted practices culminating in gross violations of human rights of protected groups, such as extrajudicial killings, torture and displacement;<br>• The specific means used to achieve "ethnic cleansing" which may underscore that the perpetration of the acts is designed to reach the foundations of the group or what is considered as such by the perpetrator group;<br>• The nature of the atrocities, e.g., dismemberment of those already killed that reveal a level of dehumanization of the group or euphoria at having total control over another human being, or the systematic rape of women which may be intended to transmit a new ethnic identity to the child or to cause humiliation and terror in order to fragment the group;<br>• The destruction of or attacks on cultural and religious property and symbols of the targeted group that may be designed to annihilate the historic presence of the group or groups;<br>• Targeted elimination of community leaders and/or men and/or women of a particular age group (the 'future generation' or a military-age group);<br>• Other practices designed to complete the exclusion of targeted group from social/political life. |

---

[4] Rome Statute of the International Criminal Court.
[5] Efforts should be made to gather information on a sufficient number of incidents to determine whether the abuses were substantial, systematic and widespread over a period of time.
[6] Deprivation of the means to sustain life can be imposed through confiscation of harvests, blockade of foodstuffs, detention in camps, forcible relocation or expulsion to inhospitable environments.

| 8. Triggering factors | *Issues to be analyzed here include:* |
|---|---|
| | Future events or circumstances seemingly unrelated to genocide that might aggravate conditions or spark deterioration in the situation, pointing to the likely onset of a genocidal episode. These 'triggers' might include: |
| | <ul><li>Upcoming elections (and associated activities such as voter registration or campaigning; revision of delimitation of electoral boundaries; a call for early elections or the postponement or cancellation of elections; disbanding of election commissions; imposition of new quotas/standards for political party or candidate eligibility);</li><li>Change of Government outside of an electoral or constitutionally sanctioned process;</li><li>Instances where the military is deployed internally to act against civilians;</li><li>Commencement of armed hostilities;</li><li>Natural disasters that may stress state capacity and strengthen active opposition groups;</li><li>Increases in opposition capacity, which may be perceived as a threat and prompt preemptive action, or rapidly declining opposition capacity which may invite rapid action to eliminate problem groups.[9]</li></ul> |

---

[7] Genocidal intent can develop gradually, e.g., in the course of conflict and not necessarily before, and genocide may be used as a "tool" or "strategy" to achieve military goals in an operation whose primary objective may be unrelated to the targeted group. Evidence of "intent to destroy" can be inferred from a set of existing facts which would suggest that what is unfolding or ongoing may be genocide. From a preventive perspective, there could be other indications of a plan or policy or an attempt to destroy a protected group before the occurrence of full-blown genocide.

[8] The hate speech has to denigrate characteristics of a specific ethnic/racial/religious/national group.

[9] Critical moments can also represent moments of opportunity to improve a situation and to lessen the risk of genocide.

# Council on Foreign Relations

Crisis Prevention

| Indicator: Electoral process/political transition | | |
|---|---|---|
| **Problem** | **Monitoring/Prevention** | **Case Study and Discussion** |
| Prone to producing violence | • UN and regional organizations such as EU, the Organization for Security and Cooperation in Europe (OSCE) provide pre-electoral technical assistance and monitoring to facilitate peaceful elections and deter improprieties.<br>• Post election international endorsement enhances winner's legitimacy or allow economic/diplomatic penalties for fraud elections.<br>• Quiet mediation by IOs with informal coalition countries helps dissuade civilian/military leaders from extra- constitutional political actions.<br>• UN lends experience to craft new constitutions during political transitions. | • Demonstrated election support in Algeria, Burundi, Kenya, Nepal, Haiti, Sri Lanka, and Ivory Coast<br>• Preventive efforts successful in Solomon Islands (2010); Lesotho and Madagascar (2009); Ghana, Kenya, and Maldives (2008); and Mauritania and Sierra Leone (2007).<br>• In 2010, UN's Office for West Africa successfully encourages military leaders in Guinea, Togo, and Niger to fulfill agreement to transfer power to civilian authorities.<br>• UN provided constitutional support to Kyrgyzstan in 2010, when president was ousted. |

Stares, Paul B, and Micah Zenko. Partnership in Preventive Action: The United States and International Institutions. Council Special Report No. 62, New York: Council on Foreign Relations, 2011.p.8-11

## Indicator: Electoral process/political transition

| Problem | Monitoring/Prevention | Case Study and Discussion |
|---|---|---|
| Prone to producing violence | • UN and regional organizations such as EU, the Organization for Security and Cooperation in Europe (OSCE) provide pre-electoral technical assistance and monitoring to facilitate peaceful elections and deter improprieties.<br>• Post election international endorsement enhances winner's legitimacy or allow economic/diplomatic penalties for fraud elections.<br>• Quiet mediation by IOs with informal coalition countries helps dissuade civilian/military leaders from extra- constitutional political actions.<br>• UN lends experience to craft new constitutions during political transitions. | • Demonstrated election support in Algeria, Burundi, Kenya, Nepal, Haiti, Sri Lanka, and Ivory Coast<br>• Preventive efforts successful in Solomon Islands (2010); Lesotho and Madagascar (2009); Ghana, Kenya, and Maldives (2008); and Mauritania and Sierra Leone (2007).<br>• In 2010, UN's Office for West Africa successfully encourages military leaders in Guinea, Togo, and Niger to fulfill agreement to transfer power to civilian authorities.<br>• UN provided constitutional support to Kyrgyzstan in 2010, when president was ousted. |

Stares, Paul B, and Micah Zenko. Partnership in Preventive Action: The United States and International Institutions. Council Special Report No. 62, New York: Council on Foreign Relations, 2011.p.8-11

## Indicator: Ethnic/religious frictions

| Problem | Monitoring/Prevention | Case Study and Discussion |
|---|---|---|
| Grievances and tensions between ethnic, minority, and religious groups turn to violence | • IOs work quietly to diffuse tensions between different ethnic and religious groups or redress grievances of specific minority groups before violence occurs.<br>• | • Work of OSCE high commissioner for minorities in addressing the discrimination toward ethnic groups in eastern and central Europe<br>• EU and the UN Assistance Mission for Iraq focused on Kosovo and the city of Kirkuk in Iraq's Kurdish region |

Stares, Paul B, and Micah Zenko. Partnership in Preventive Action: The United States and International Institutions. Council Special Report No. 62, New York: Council on Foreign Relations, 2011.p.8-11

| Indicator: Boundary/territorial disputes | | |
| --- | --- | --- |
| **Problem** | **Monitoring/Prevention** | **Case Study and Discussion** |
| Land and maritime border disputes erupts into violence | • Arbitrate land and maritime disputes<br>• Monitor precious and contested resources between borders<br>• Preventive boundary/territorial dispute resolution and monitoring | • In 2010, UN's International Court of Justice and UN's Office for West Africa adjudicated border dispute about recent discovery of oil deposits involving Cameroon and Nigeria<br>• UN's regional Center for Preventive Diplomancy for Central Asia help resolve water rights in the region.<br>• OAS mediated border dispute between Belize and Guatemala<br>• Association of Southeast Asian Nations (ASEAN) brokered and observed border conflict between Cambodia and Thailand |

Stares, Paul B, and Micah Zenko. Partnership in Preventive Action: The United States and International Institutions. Council Special Report No. 62, New York: Council on Foreign Relations, 2011.p.8-11

| Indicator: Resource/food scarcity | | |
| --- | --- | --- |
| **Problem** | **Monitoring/Prevention** | **Case Study and Discussion** |
| Shocks in price spikes, food shortages, or natural disasters can trigger political unrest and violence | • Monitor food pricing, shortages<br>• Prepare for natural disasters<br>• Forecast humanitarian early warnings for natural hazards that precede food shortages | • World Bank and IMF have contingent emergency loans and flexible credit lines for resource, food scarcity, and natural disasters<br>• UN World Food Program operates the Inter-Agency Standing Committee on Humanitarian Early Warning Service, providing early warnings and forecasts for natural hazards preceding food shortages |

Stares, Paul B, and Micah Zenko. Partnership in Preventive Action: The United States and International Institutions. Council Special Report No. 62, New York: Council on Foreign Relations, 2011.p.8-11

# APPENDIX F

Analysis of Third Party Early Warning Signs and Purpose:

| THIRD PARTY ORG | EARLY WARNING | PURPOSE |
|---|---|---|
| United Nations, Special Advisor on the Prevention of Genocide | 1. Inter-group relations, including record of discrimination and/or other human rights violations committed against a group<br>2. Circumstances that affect the capacity to prevent genocide<br>3. Presence of illegal arms and armed elements<br>4. Motivation of leading actors in the State/region; acts which serve to encourage divisions between national, racial, ethnic, and religious groups<br>5. Circumstances that facilitate perpetration of genocide (dynamic factors)<br>6. Genocidal acts<br>7. Evidence of intent "to destroy in whole or in part<br>8.Triggers<br>Upcoming elections (and associated activities such as voter registration or campaigning; revision of delimitation of electoral boundaries; a call for early elections or the postponement or cancellation of elections; disbanding of election commissions; imposition of new quotas/standards for political party or candidate eligibility);<br>• Change of Government outside of an electoral or constitutionally sanctioned process;<br>• Instances where the military is deployed internally to act against civilians;<br>• Commencement of armed hostilities;<br>• Natural disasters that may stress state capacity and strengthen active opposition groups;<br>• Increases in opposition capacity, which may be perceived as a threat and prompt preemptive action, or rapidly declining opposition capacity which may invite rapid | Ultimately, the role of early warnings and indicators work to assist with prevention of genocide and mass atrocities in three areas: raising awareness; alerting; and advocacy.<br><br>"Eliminating gross political and economic inequalities, and promoting a common sense of belonging on equal footing."[224]<br><br>"Decisions about collective action, as well as judgments about whether peaceful means are inadequate and whether "national authorities are manifestly failing to protect," should ultimately be made by the Security Council or, less frequently, by the General Assembly. Such decisions, however, are normally informed, at least in part, by information and assessments provided by the Secretariat, especially if they are to be taken "in a timely and decisive manner," as called for in the World Summit Outcome. In such cases, the quality and timeliness of the inputs from the Secretariat are vital, especially to those Member States that do not have extensive national sources of information and analysis."[225] |

| | | |
|---|---|---|
| | action to eliminate problem groups."[223] | |
| Sentinel Satellite Project | Possible threats to civilians and evidence of pending mass violence. "warning signs — elevated roads for moving heavy armor, lengthened airstrips for landing attack aircraft, build-ups of troops, tanks, and artillery preparing for invasion"[226] | Alert public, the press, policymakers, major news organizations, and social media; especially, Twitter and Facebook. The stated purpose is to observe alleged atrocity as it develops and unfolds and to "document, deter, and seek accountability for war criminals and mass atrocities."[227] |
| UNOSAT | 1. Preliminary reporting of conflict zones or areas of interest[228] 2. Damaged and/or destroyed buildings to including hospitals, schools, residential neighborhoods, and cultural and religious sites. Populations considered under threat and militia deployments.[229] "UNOSAT is designed to produce concrete output for identified users and beneficiaries by turning technology into concrete and usable applications for UN agencies, member states, and communities in a variety of areas. UNOSAT addresses three main homogeneous user systems: Humanitarian Affairs and Relief Coordination (Crisis & Situational Mapping, Damage and Impact Assessment, Human Security); Monitoring (Safety and Security, Human Rights, Territorial Planning and Monitoring); [and] Capacity Development & Technical Assistance (In-country Project Development & Implementation)."[230] | Our goal is to make satellite solutions and geographic information easily accessible to the UN family and to experts worldwide who work at reducing the impact of crises and disasters and help nations plan for sustainable development."[231] UNOSAT believed that geographic analysis positively affects "processes, initiatives and organizations with a mission to protect human rights and uphold international humanitarian law, thus improving overall human security internationally."[232] The contribution of the system has human security application in these five areas: • Advocacy • Mitigation and Prevention • Enhancing Field Investigations • Remote Fact Finding • Peace and Reconciliation[233] |

[224]Office of the Special Adviser on the Prevention of Genocide.

[225]United Nations General Assembly, 2.

[223]Office of the Special Adviser on the Prevention of Genocide.

[226]Satellite Sentinel Project, *Documenting the Crisis*.

[227]Ibid.

[228]United Nations Institute for Training and Research, UNOSAT Brief, 9.

[229]Ibid.

[230]United Nations Institute for Training and Research, *What We Do*.

[231]United Nations Institute for Training and Research, *Who We Are*.

| WITNESS | "WITNESS empowers human rights defenders to use video to fight injustice, and to transform personal stories of abuse into powerful tools that can pressure those in power or with power to act."[234] They bridge a gap between media, human rights, and technology by using innovation to the traditional approaches to advocacy. [235] | 1. Activism, a tool for change, [236] 2. Empower and expose injustice. Empower activists to protect and defend human rights.[237] 3. Document human rights violations.[238] 4. Ensure transparency, good governance, and accountability are upheld within society. [239] 5. "WITNESS' unique contribution to the human rights community is to serve as global authority on best practices in the use of video for human rights purposes and a frontline resource for training and expertise."[240] |
|---|---|---|
| Amnesty International | Observes Human Rights Violations based upon the Universal Declaration of Human Rights[241] | 1. To unite people to fight for human rights using three tactics: research; action; and advocacy. 2. Publishes independent reports based upon rigorous research, undisturbed by corporate and government influence. 3. Using campaigns and long-term casework to influence human rights concerns using stories of at-risk individuals to the international media. 4. Hold the attention of government officials, policy makers, corporations, and international institutions. 5. As advocates, Amnesty promotes legislation and policies to advance human rights by integrating media and grassroots mobilization that |

---

[232]United Nations Institute for Training and Research, *UNOSAT Brief,* 5.

[233]Ibid.

[234]WITNESS, "About Us: Our Mission."

[235]Ibid.

[236]WITNESS, *Cameras Everywhere: Current challenges and opportunities at the intersection of human rights, video and technology,* 8.

[237]Ibid.

[238]Ibid., 10.

[239]Ibid.

[240]WITNESS, "About Us: Our Mission."

[241]Amnesty International, "About Us: Mission."

| | | assists to protect individuals and free prisoners of conscience.[242] |
|---|---|---|
| FEWER | 1. Conflict and peace generating factors[243]<br>2. Root causes, proximate causes, and triggers of conflict, peace indicators, and stakeholder analysis of interests, agendas, and capacities[244] | "Analysis on conflict dynamics for practical use by policy-makers." [245]<br>"Ensure that local, regional and international actors participate in and 'own' conflict prevention and peacebuilding activities."[246]<br>Early warning and response systems base upon: systematic training and capacity building; conflict monitoring, analysis, and reporting; policy response and strategy development; and to raise awareness. [247] |
| FIDH | 1. Violations of the **Universal Declaration of Human Rights**<br>2. Fact Finding Missions able to view the violations of UDHR.<br>3. Countries in transition that might resume conflict<br>4. Countries facing new elections after conflict[248] | Defends civil, political, economic and cultural rights, established from the **Universal Declaration of Human Rights**, acting in legal and political fields for implementation of international instruments to protect human rights and for human rights implementation. A federalist movement acting through national member and partner organizations working with local civil societies to identify local obstacles and mobilize support to overcome them.[249] |
| Human Rights Watch | 1. Investigations of violations of international human rights laws.[250]<br>2. Refugee Camp interviews, military and rebel outpost interviews, and satellite imagery information [251] | 1. Defend and protect human rights.[252]<br>2. Support the oppressed and hold perpetrators accountable for crimes.[253]<br>3. Production of rigorous and |

[242]Ibid.

[243]FEWER. "Early Warning Early Response."

[244]Ibid.

[245]FEWER. "FEWER Africa." 

[246]Ibid.

[247]FEWER. "Early Warning Early Response."

[248]FIDH, *Annual Report 2010,* 4.

[249]Ibid.

[250]Human Rights Watch, "About Us."

[251]Human Rights Watch, "Methodology."

[252]Human Rights Watch. "About Us."

[253]Ibid.

| | | |
|---|---|---|
| | | objective investigations. [254]<br>4. Build strategic and targeted advocacy with intense pressure for action. [255]<br>5. Change legal and moral structures for a change for better justice and security for everyone in the world [256]<br>6. Prevent discrimination by supporting victims and activists, uphold political freedom, protect people from inhumane wartime conduct, and to bring justice to perpetrators. [257]<br>7. Investigate and expose human rights violations; holding abusers accountable. [258]<br>8. Challenge governments and power brokers to end abusive practices and respect international human rights law. [259]<br>9. Enlist the support of the public and international community for human rights for everyone[260] |
| International Crisis Group | ICG reports on conflict prevention and resolution across the world for issues dealing with Islamist terrorism, nuclear proliferation, local conflict issues, and problems dealing with failed, failing, and fragile states. [261]<br>Conflict as it pertains to the deterioration of Peace and Justice, Gender, Climate Change, and the Responsibility to Protect.[262] | 1. Production of analytical reports with recommendations for key international decision makers.<br>2. Publication of Crisis Watch Bulletin, providing regular updates on significant or potential conflicts in the world.<br>3. Generate support from governments and the media for policy prescription to conflict.<br>4. Using reports, the Crisis Group Board, makes recommendations to senior policy makers around the world. [263] |

[254]Ibid.

[255]Ibid.

[256]Ibid.

[257]Ibid.

[258]Ibid.

[259]Ibid.

[260]Human Rights Watch, "About Us."

[261]International Crisis Group, "About Crisis Group."

[262] International Crisis Group, "Key Issues."

[263] International Crisis Group, Asia Report No. 204, 21.

| Genocide Watch | Prediction uses models such as Dr. Stanton's "Eight Stages of Genocide" as an instrument to analyze situations for educational, policy analysis, and advocacy purposes. [264] | Genocide Watch has objectives in education, prediction, prevention, intervention, and justice. "Genocide Watch exists to predict, prevent, stop, and punish genocide and other forms of mass murder. We seek to raise awareness and influence public policy concerning potential and actual genocide. Our purpose is to build an international movement to prevent and stop genocide." [265] |

---

[264] Genocide Watch, "About Us."

[265] Ibid.

# BIBLIOGRAPHY

Albright, Madeleine K. and William S. Cohen. *Preventing Genocide: A Blueprint for U.S. Policymakers.* Washington, DC: United States Holocaust Memorial Museum, The American Academy of Diplocacy, and the Endowment of the United States Institute of Peace, 2008.

_____. *United States Institute for Peace.* 4 August 2011, http://www.usip.org/joint-statement-mass-atrocities (accessed 15 March 2012).

Amnesty International. "News: Syria: From all-out repression to armed conflict in Aleppo." August 15, 2012. http://www.amnesty.org/en/news/syria-all-out-repression-armed-conflict-aleppo-2012-08-01 (accessed August 15, 2012).Amnesty International. "Science for Human Rights." http://www.amnestyusa.org/research/ science-for-human-rights (accessed 17 August 2012).

_____. "About Us: Mission." http://www.amnestyusa.org/about-us/our-mission (accessed 15 August 2012).

_____. "Eyes on Darfur." 15 August 2012, http://www.amnestyusa.org/research/ science-for-human-rights/eyes-on-darfur (accessed 15 August 2012).

Appleman, Roy E. "South to the Naktong, North to the Yalu (June-November 1950)." *Center of Military History United States Army*, 1992: 20-21.

Bellamy, Alex J. *Mass Atrocities and Armed Conflict: Links, Distinctions, and Implications for the Responsibility to Prevent.* Muscatine, IA: The Stanley Foundation, 2011.

Branham, Lindsay and Jocelyn Kelly. *We Suffer From War and More War: Assessment Of The Impact Of The Lord's Resistance Army On Formerly Abducted Children and Their CommunitiesIn Northeastern Democratic Republic Of The Congo.* DTJ Publications, 2012.

Buchanan, Tom. "NATO, Britain, France and the FRG. Nuclear Strategies and Forces for Europe. 1949-2000 by Beatrice Heuser." *The English Historical Review*, 2000: 263-264.

Carpenter, Ted Galen. *Smart Power: Toward a Prudent Foreign Policy for America.* Washington, DC: Cato Institute, 2008.

Coyle, Diane and Patrick Meier. *New Technologies in Emergencies and Conflicts: The Role of Information and Social Networks.* Washington, DC: UN Foundation-Vodafone Foundation Partnership, 2009.

Department of Defense. *Joint Operational Access Concept (JOAC).* Concept, White Paper, Washington, DC: Department of Defense, 2012.

EyesonDarfur. "Eyes on Darfur." 15 August 2012. http://www.eyesondarfur.org/satellite.html (accessed 15 August 2012).

Feinstein, Lee. "Darfur and Beyond: What Is Needed to Prevent Mass Atrocities." *Council Special Report.* New York: Council on Foreign Relations, 2007.

FEWER. "Early Warning Early Response." http://www.fewer-international.org/pages/africa/projects_14.html (accessed 16 August 2012).

_____. "FEWER Africa." http://www.fewer-international.org/pages/africa/ (accessed 16 August 2012).

FIDH. *Annual Report 2010.* Paris: FIDH, 2010.

General Assembly Security Council. A/65/877-S/2022/393. *The role of regional and subregional arrangements in implementing the responsibility to protect.* General Assembly, 65th Sess. (New York: United Nations, 2011).

Genocide Watch. "About Us." http://www.genocidewatch.org/aboutus/ missionstatement.html (accessed 18 August 2012).

Goldhagen, Daniel Jonah. *Worse Than War: Genocide, Eliminationism, and the Ongoing Assault on Humanity.* New York: Public Affairs, 2009.

Hamburg, David A. *Preventing Genocide: Practical Steps Toward Early Detection and Effective Action.* Boulder, CO: Paradigm Publishers, 2008.

Harvard Humanitarian Initiative. *Escalation: Evidence of the SAF and SPLA Combat Operations.* Human Security Incident Report, Satellite Sentinel Project, 2012.

_____. "Harvard Humanitarian Initiative." http://www.hhi.harvard.edu/ (accessed 17 July 2012).

Headquarters, Department of the Army. ADP 3-0. *Unified Land Operations.* Washington, DC: Government Printing Office, 2011.

_____. ADP 5-0. *The Operations Process.* Washington, DC: Government Printing Office, 2012.

_____.Field Manual (FM 5-0). *Army Doctrine Publication.* Washington, DC: Government Printing Office, 2010.

Human Rights Watch. "Methodology." http://www.hrw.org/node/75141 (accessed August 10, 2010).

_____. "About Us." http://www.hrw.org/about (accessed 10 August 2010).

International Commission on Intervention and State Sovereignty. "The Responsibility to Protect." *Report.* Ottawa, ON, Canada: International Development Research Centre, 2001.

_____. *The Responsibility to Protect. Right of Humanitarian Intervention.* Ottawa: International Development Research Centre, 2001.

International Crisis Group. "About Crisis Group." http://www.crisisgroup.org/en/about.aspx (accessed 18 August 2012).

_____. "Key Issues." http://www.crisisgroup.org/en/publication-type/key-issues.aspx (accessed 20 August 2012).

_____. Asia Report No. 204. *Tajinkistan: The Changing Insurgent Threats* Washington, DC: International Crisis Group, 2011.

James T. White & Company. *The National Cyclopaedia of American Biography.* New York: James T. White & Company, 1897.

Joint Chiefs of Staff. Joint Publication 5-0. *Joint Operations Planning.* Washington, DC: Government Printing Office, 2011.

Meier, Patrick, and Jennifer Leaning. *Applying Technology to Crisis Mapping and Early Warning in Humanitarian Settings.* Cambridge, MA: Harvard Humanitarian Initiative, 2009.

Obama, Barack. *Letter from the President to Speaker of House Regarding the Commencement of Operations in Libya.* Washington, DC: The White House, Office of the Press Secretary, 2011.

_____. *Letter from the President to the Speaker of the House and the President Pro-Tempore of the Senate Regarding the Lord's Resistance Army.* Washington, DC: Office of the Press Secretary, 14 October 2011.

_____. *National Security Strategy.* Washington, DC: The White House, 2010.

_____. *Presidential Study Directive on Mass Atrocities.* August 2011, http://www.whitehouse.gov/the-press-office/2011/08/04/presidential-study-directive-mass-atrocities (accessed 27 February 2012).

_____. *Letter from the President regarding the commencement of operations in Libya.* 21 March 2011. http://www.whitehouse.gov/the-press-office/2011/03/21/letter-president-regarding-commencement-operations-libya (accessed 27 February 2012).

_____. *Presidential Study Directive on Mass Atrocities.* August 2011. http://www.whitehouse.gov/the-press-office/2011/08/04/presidential-study-directive-mass-atrocities (accessed 27 February 2012).

Office of the UN Special Adviser on the Prevention of Gencode, "Overview of OSAPG." http://www.un.org/en/preventgenocide/adviser/pdf/osapg_overview.pdf (accessed 16 August 2012).

Satellite Sentinel Project. "Documenting the Crisis." http://satsentinel.org/documenting-the-crisis, (accessed 3 August 2012).

_____. "Our Story." http://satsentinel.org/our-story/partner-organizations#enough (accessed 3 August 2012).

_____. *Seige: Evidence of Encirclement of the Kauda Valley 25 January 2012.* Human Rights Violations, Harvard: Harvard Humanitarian Institute, 2012.

School of Advanced Military Studies. *Art of Design: Student Text, Version 2.0.* Fort Leavenworth: School of Advanced Military Studies, 2010.

Shaw, Martin. *War & Genocide.* Cambridge, MA: Polity Press, 2003.

Stanton, Gregory H. "The 8 Stages of Genocide," *Genocide Watch,* http://www.genocidewatch.org/aboutgenocide/8stagesofgenocide.html, 1998 (accessed 27 June 2012).

Stares, Paul B. and Micahl Zenko. Council Special Report No. 62. *Partnership in Preventive Action: The United States and International Institutions.* New York: Council on Foreign Relations, 2011.

U.S. Army Peacekeeping and Stability Operations Institute. *Mass Atrocity Prevention and Response Options (MAPRO): A Policy Planning Handbook.* Carlisle: Peacekeeping and Stability Operations Institute, 2012.

United Nations General Assembly. *Early Warning, Assessment and the Responsibility to Protect.* Sixty-fourth session, Agenda items 48 and 114, A/64/864. New York: United Nations Assembly, 2010.

United Nations Institute for Training and Research. *AT Brief: Satellite Applications for Human Security.* Washington, DC: UNITAR, 2011.

_____.United Nations Institute for Training and Research. *UNOSAT Brief: Satellite Applications for Human Security.* Washington, DC: UNITAR, 2011.

_____. *What We Do.* http://www.unitar.org/unosat/what-we-do (accessed 19 August 2012).

_____.*Who We Are.* http://www.unitar.org/unosat/who-we-are (accessed 4 August 2012).

United Nations, Security Council, SC 10200. *'No-Fly Zone' Over Libya, Authorizing All Necessary Measures to Protect Civilians,* 6498th Meeting. New York: United Nations, 2011.

WITNESS. "About Us: Our Mission." http://www.witness.org/about-us (accessed 12 August 2012).

_____. *Cameras Everywhere: Current challenges and opportunities at the intersection of human rights, video and technology. Human Rights Video and Technology.* Brooklyn: WITNESS, 2011.

_____. *Video for Change Toolkit.* http://videoplan.witness.org/en/about/witness-methodology (accessed 13 August 2012).

Woocher, Lawrence. *Unitest States Institute of Peace.* March 29, 2011. http://www.usip.org/publications/libya-genocide-prevention-and-the-responsibility-protect (accessed 15 March 2012).